Running Away From Home

To Amy

A souvenir from the old man who accompanied you to Malaysia in 2013

Running Away From Home

Stories collected by

David Syme

With best wishes

David

DB

DIADEM BOOKS

RUNNING AWAY FROM HOME

Published by Diadem Books
Distribution coordination by Spiderwize

For information, please contact:

Diadem Books
Mews Cottage
The Causeway
KENNOWAY
Kingdom of Fife
KY8 5JU
Scotland UK

www.diadembooks.com

ISBN: 978-1-908026-00-2

Every morning in Africa, a gazelle wakes up.
It knows it must outrun the fastest lion or it will be killed.
Every morning in Africa, a lion wakes up.
It knows that it must run faster than the slowest gazelle, or it will starve.
It doesn't matter whether you're a lion or a gazelle
when the sun comes up you'd better be running.
(But, unless you're a runner, you won't understand.)

Anon

Table of Contents

UNITED KINGDOM

EUROPE

AMERICAS

Acknowledgements

I would like to thank my fellow contributors for their enthusiastic co-operation in this project, also Helen Rainbow for the first editorial read and positive support. Joanne of Diadem Books has been a sympathetic and knowledgeable partner in the production of the book and I would like to thank my wife Pat for putting up with my penchant for "interesting" runs over the years.

Introduction

THESE SHORT STORIES are for all runners who enjoy running away from their normal routes. It could be a race, a run with family or friends or a solo run in a new location, there is always a thrill of exploration to spice up the run! The contributors are all runners whose first move in packing for a journey is to put the full running kit into the case.

Work has taken me to many countries, and I have travelled widely with friends and family on holiday. My son Andrew Syme lives in Garmisch-Partenkirchen, Germany, and is a top mountain-runner there, while my daughter Fiona Syme has inherited my interest in marathons in exotic locations. Frank Tooley and Paul Houston are leading members of my running club, Harmeny Athletic, and share our passion for the adventurous run. We have all enjoyed writing down our experiences to earn some money for a deserving charity; perhaps our readers also have stories which could appear in a second volume? Please send contributions to: runafh2010@hotmail.com

David Syme

My First Time...

David

David with sister-in-law Margaret at Lake Louise
(see "Living the Dream" page 106)

IN 1982 I WAS WORKING as Senior Education Officer at the Scottish Infantry Depot, Bridge of Don. The barracks were just outside Aberdeen near the coast where the skirl of the pipes from the Army School of Piping competed with the cry of sea birds, and the biting easterly winds chilled the blood.

The Commanding Officer's conference one February morning took its usual course, but the last item caught me out.   One Company Commander told the Commanding Officer, Lieutenant Colonel Richard Cross, that some of his Corporals wanted to take part in the Aberdeen Milk Marathon in September, and that they requested time off for training.   The CO thought for a moment, then decreed that they could, as long as an officer supervised them in training and at the event.   As I was the last officer to dive under the table I was nominated Officer in Charge of Marathon Training.   It was made clear to me by all present that the best way to carry out this task was to run the thing myself.

Looking back, I see this as a fortunate development in my sporting life.   I was a lumbering rugby prop forward with a keen appetite for beer, and as I entered my 40s should have been considering a different sport anyway.   But running?   I was not built for speed, and had never tried a long run.   I shared my concern with my fellow prop as we laced up our boots for a game.

"If you do it, I'll do it!" said Sergeant "Ozzie" Osborne of the King's Own Scottish Borderers.   We shook hands on it, and I set about entry forms and a training schedule.   I had ten Corporals, Ozzie, fellow-educators Captains David Hopwood, Alan Munro and myself.   The Corporals and the Captains were all fit young thrusters, so I sensibly chose to act as training facilitator rather than trainer, and my plan was that we trained together every Thursday afternoon; additional training would be individual responsibility.

Our joint training on Thursdays was simple.   To the west of the Barracks lay a network of minor roads through rolling farmland.   We took a minibus to a start point and ran back to the barracks, each week increasing the distance until we topped out at 20 miles. The fact that transport for this training turned up without a hiccough was due to the fact that Ozzie was in charge of motor transport at the Depot! He and I were always last home, and we checked with the guardroom that all the other runners had reported in. Aberdeen University's Medical School asked us if we would assist with an experiment, so we supplied blood and urine samples and had body temperature taken before and after each training run, and before and after the race itself. The experiment showed that runners taking electrolyte drinks performed no better than those taking plain water.

Novice marathon runners will perhaps identify with my anxiety as the date for the race approached. I had been exhausted after the longer training runs—how would I cope with the full distance in a competition? Then I had a flash of inspiration! My wife had taken the children south to stay with her parents for a few days. On a late Friday evening I drove to the race start/finish at the Beach Boulevard, parked up, then walked and jogged gently round the entire course. It took me five and a half hours, but I was jubilant! I had not been racing, so was relaxed. I had enjoyed seeing Aberdeen and lower Deeside in the wee small hours. Most important, the obstacle of 26 miles in my mind was demolished. I knew that I could run much faster and still avoid the potential disappointment of dropping out.

On the day itself I relished the pre-race buzz, started slowly and found a good rhythm. My confidence kept me buoyant, even on the long rural stretches with few spectators or fellow-competitors, only a lonely piper at every crossroad. At the 20-mile mark I caught up with Ozzie, who was struggling, and we ran the last part together, finishing in 4.32.

It was definitely "The First Time" for me, and that huge post-race sense of achievement has never left me. Twenty-eight years on and running is still an important part of my life; I run wherever I go and still enter races now and then.

Thank you, Richard Cross!

My First Time...

Frank

Frank during triathlon training

RUNNING WAS AN IMPORTANT PART OF PE at my High School: Lenzie Academy.

When the Gym Teacher couldn't be bothered to teach, he just set the classes off to run 'The Mile', a relatively flat 2.5 mile course on pavements and a rough path beside the Glasgow-Edinburgh railway. This conveniently took a 'period' to complete with changing and showers after. We all hated it, except my good friend, Graham Williamson, who went on to beat Steve Cram on several occasions; he still holds, amongst others, the Scottish 1 mile record.

I rediscovered running in 2006 when I had to stand in for my injured wife in a 5-mile leg of the Hairy Haggis Edinburgh Marathon relay. I ran the 2nd leg and recall waiting in a park in Edinburgh for my wife's boss to tag me, clutching my asthma inhaler and unsure what to wear, what pace to run or even whether I would be able to run such a long distance or would need to walk part of it.

Four years later, I run that distance at lunch times 3-4 times a week.

My First Time...

Fiona

Fiona with No 2 son Finley

IT HAD BEEN a very enjoyable first term at University. The freedom of being there and eating what I wanted and when I wanted it suited me, sleeping late (when not at lectures of course!), socialising into the wee hours and discovering the Students' Union happy hours offer of £1 a pint felt like heaven!

However, on returning home for Christmas I was soon to realise that all these indulgencies had taken a visible toll on me. The clothes in my wardrobe at home all felt a little tighter than I'd remembered, family Christmas Day photographs revealed a rather round looking face with the hint of a double chin and my Dad described me to someone on the phone as "a little heavier than she used to be!"

Something had to be done quickly so I asked my Dad to help me get fit and shed a few pounds before returning to University for the Easter term. A "boot camp" running programme was promptly drawn up with a healthy eating plan, and off we went with great enthusiasm.

After only a week of fairly short and gentle runs I was feeling fitter and, more importantly, was thoroughly enjoying my new way of life. By the time I returned to university I had shed a few pounds, was a picture of health and excited about sharing my new fitness regime with my flatmates.

I soon realised that the benefits of running were so much greater than simply the weight loss I was enjoying. Suddenly I found getting out of bed much easier, I had a spring in my step and most of all was exploring parts of Glasgow I would otherwise have never come across. I got a great thrill from discovering a riverside path I didn't know existed or coming across a park or footpath in a new area, and I started to see running as an escape from the daily grind of lectures and assignments that comes with being a student.

On graduating from University I spent a year doing a lot of travelling across Europe and made sure the first things that went into my rucksack were my trainers and, in fact, I still do the same now whenever I go on holiday.

Numerous 10km races, 14 half marathons and 12 full marathons later I look back on those £1 pints and feel they did me a huge favour. I may never have discovered the joy of running without them!

My First Time...

Andrew

Andrew with winner's trophy, Osterfelder Mountain Race
(see p. 44)

DOES ANYONE ELSE REMEMBER the first time when somewhere in our heads it went "click"—and suddenly it became clear what this whole running business is about?

My Dad, a keen runner, had always tried to introduce me to the joys of running but I just couldn't see the point of it at all. I would run if there was a ball of any size or colour to chase but simply to run was boring.

I'd like to share with you the first time it went "click" with me. It qualifies for *Running Away From Home* because it happened when I was at boarding school.

It was March 1985; I was 14 years old and standing on a rugby pitch, soaked to the skin and freezing cold. The occasion was the annual school cross-country race and most of us had dreaded this day for several weeks; well, to be precise, the last 52 weeks. Our aim was to get around the 6km course without too much effort or pain but to still achieve a respectable finishing place and so avoiding merciless slagging for the next year.

Of course, as always, the weather was at its worst. It was one of those days when you stayed at home unless you had to go out, for example if your house was burning. The temperature was slightly above zero, it was sleeting heavily but the worst aspect was the numbing gale-force wind which battered our faces.

So there we were, about 150 boys standing in this rugby field huddled together, heads dipped in communal, frozen misery similar to penguins during a snowstorm down in the Antarctic. We had on only our rugby tops, shorts and shoes more suited for squash or badminton. At the start I had strategically placed myself about two thirds down the starting field.

After much delay the school's sports teacher finally appeared, all wrapped up in weatherproof clothing, armed with his starting pistol. "On your marks, get set…" Nothing! His gun didn't fire, and it took him several minutes to work out the problem with his gun; then finally we were off!

I took two strides, then realised my shoelaces were undone. How stupid! With all that time I hadn't glanced down and checked them—beginner's mistake! I knelt down to tie them, which was easier said than done with numb fingers; I stood up and realised to my horror that I was in the very last position. Even the somewhat overweight complete non-sporty fellow pupils were waddling ahead of me! Spurred on by the thought of being the joke of the class for a whole year, I sprinted off to get back to the area in the field I wanted to be in. After a few minutes I'd overtaken quite a few and decided to continue with the pace. I was enjoying overtaking people and the speed meant I was warming up as blood started to circulate around other parts of my body apart from my vital organs! At about the 4th kilometre we ran up the side of a steep field. Most of the other boys walked this part but I kept on running and found myself even overtaking some of the "heroes" of the school, the 1st team rugby players.

Towards the end I ran out of steam, but I held my position and finished in the top twenty.

And so the seeds were sown; I didn't immediately become a runner but it was certainly a turning point in my attitude towards running and, for me, the moment when my "click" happened!

My First Time...

Paul

Paul running the Perth Ultrafest 2010
(picture by roadrunpics.com)

MY **FIRST TASTE** of running came in 2007. I had just finished University and, as well as a degree, I also had a good few extra pounds around my midsection to show for my four years of being a student! I started to get a little more active and joined a gym. I would mainly use the cross-trainer and rowing machine and I would absolutely stay away from the treadmill!

After a few months, I was roped into running the Great Edinburgh Run 2007 by my employers for charity. I say roped in, but I actually volunteered, thinking that it was five months away so I didn't have to worry about it—a mentality that still persists in me to this day!

With five months to go, I still hadn't run outside at all and the first few ventures outdoors were a bit of an ordeal. I probably wouldn't have kept it up past a week if I didn't have the race to focus on. I started out running a mile or so at a time. After a few weeks, I was running a few miles every time, and after a couple of months I was delighted to be able to finish a 5-mile long run in just under an hour! 5 miles was the furthest I would run before the race.

With a week to go before the race, I was seriously starting to regret my decision to enter five months previously—again, something that still occurs to this day! 10k seemed like a marathon to me. But nothing could have prepared me for the feeling on the day. With the sheer number of runners and spectators all around the course, I felt a huge surge of adrenaline all the way round. It wasn't easy (especially running around a windy Arthur's Seat) but I'll always remember the feeling of getting past mile 5, knowing that this was the furthest I'd ever run and that I was still strong and a lot faster than I'd ever been. I finished my first 10k in 46:40.

After crossing the line, I felt my first competitive instincts kick in. I thought, if only I'd started out a bit faster, or if I hadn't stopped to have a drink half way round, I could maybe have been under 45 minutes. I knew then that I'd be doing it again! One week later, I joined Harmeny Athletic Club. The benefit you get from running with other, faster people cannot be underestimated and within a couple of months I was running 10ks in under 40 minutes and was well and truly hooked.

The rest, as they say...

UNITED KINGDOM

A Run Through the Capital

David

THE 27th LONDON MARATHON took place on Sunday 22 April 2007. I took part as a club runner representing Harmeny Athletic Club, near Edinburgh, after a coin toss in December 06 for the club's last remaining place. Training had been good, mainly with club members who were training for the Paris Marathon which was run one week before London. We had "put in the miles" and I hoped to finish at 4hrs 15 mins or so.

My wife Pat and I flew down to London on Saturday 21st. We had been warned about the crowds at Marathon Registration in Excel, so Pat went straight to our hotel while I braved the throng. There were queues to do everything, many queues consisting of runners and their entire families! I shuffled forward to collect my number, shuffled again to get my time chip, and was pushed gently by the flow round the exhibition stands, none of which looked very attractive by this late stage. Queuing again for a pasta meal was one queue too many, so I picked up a goody bag and headed back for a quiet night. Installed in our hotel room, I rummaged through the free samples in the goody bag. I mistook the shower gel for skin cream, and rubbed a large dollop into my face (in anticipation of a sunny day for the run). My face soon started to throb, so I washed it off quickly enough! After a pasta meal and a stroll round

Marble Arch I laid out all my kit for the run and settled in for a long, passive evening of watching snooker and Match of the Day. The TV weather forecast was excellent—clear sky and no wind.

I awoke at 6 after quite a good night, and dressed carefully. I had trained frequently in these clothes; all were trusted old friends. It was already quite warm, so rather than use the Marathon clothing bag, I put a small plastic bag with some money into my pocket and carried only a bottle of water. Breakfast was taken in the bedroom; this was simply a Soreen malt loaf and an energy fruit drink. With sleepy "Good luck" wishes in my ear I set off in good time.

I felt conspicuous walking to the tube station with running kit and number, but the platform and trains were full of runners (and their families) so I was just another runner from then on. From Marble Arch to Bond Street was crowded, from Bond Street to Charing Cross more so, but from Charing Cross to Blackheath was chaos! There was a buzz of excited chatter in my carriage. I was wedged next to Damien, an Australian living in Putney who was running his second marathon, but had his eye on the Comrades Marathon later this year. He hoped to finish in 4 hours. The walk from the station was a welcome chance for our train-load to stretch out and relax, then we divided into red and blue starts. The holding area for "runners-only" was vast and empty, and it was very pleasant to wander around in the fresh morning sunshine. Toilet facilities were excellent, drinking water plentiful and the voice on the loudspeaker system not too excited. I missed my son and daughter at this stage, as we had run several marathons together, and most of the other runners were in groups.

The race was due to start at 0945hrs, and at 0900hrs they opened the start pens. I was the first into Pen 8, so sat at the very front. I chatted to a young lad from Blackheath, whose wife's first baby was overdue. He had a mobile strapped to his arm in case of any development. Being so far back we missed the pre-start chat and warm-up (if there was one) and only faintly heard the start, which was done by Mary Peters (I remember her) and Ronan Keating (who he?). Of course nothing happened for a while for us, then we shuffled forward, crossing the start almost 9 minutes after the gun.

Boy! Was it good to be running! Sadly we were down to walking pace after a minute or so, and had to walk through a bottle-neck for 2-3 minutes before daylight appeared between us and the runners in front. Even in the first few miles it was clear that many had overstated their ability on the entry form and had been penned too near the front; some were walking after 2 miles, others were in it for laughs, even at this early stage milking the crowd and making phone calls. At this point I would say that the most negative aspect of this event was the constant need to overtake; to weave in and out of slower runners and walkers (even although I had to walk at the end). I was one of the few runners at my level not wearing a charity vest, and this is the lesson I learned. For a runner of my humble ability London is not to be taken too seriously. Train hard for the 26 miles, of course, but dress up, chase some sponsorship and raise money for a good cause, and, above all, enjoy the terrific atmosphere.

I chatted up a lady alongside me with the unlikely line: "Excellent water stops here, aren't there" and we talked for a while. She came from Nottingham and was another non-charity runner. She said that she enjoyed running behind me, because she "liked my running line." She kept on my heels for most of the course, to my astonishment. One moment I was up on the kerb, then squeezing between groups, ducking and diving, yet she kept right behind me! We parted when she joined a queue for a toilet. I also chatted up a Serviceman raising money for the Airborne Forces Association, and ran alongside a huge bottle of Lucozade being worn by Lisa—"Come on Lisa!" "Well done, Lisa!" I heard this from the enthusiastic crowd for much of the route. The spectators offered sweets, oranges, chocolate and little hands to be touched. Many runners had their names on their clothing, and they, like Lisa, received individual encouragement. Eventually I left Lisa behind, but could not overtake the heavily-perspiring Scooby-doo.

Pat and our daughter Fiona had told me to look out for them at miles 11 and 21, and I was looking forward to some support. Mile 11 came and went with no sign of them, but I saw Fiona at mile 21. I learned later that I had passed within 2 feet of them at mile 12, which was as close as they could reach to mile 11. They had screamed my name, but I had missed them. Going too fast, I suppose. I also saw nephews John and James with their wives Caroline and Rachel, and, at mile 25, Anne, who had been on an expedition with me to Venezuela. (Stopped for a little chat on the last two occasions, so could justify taking a minute or two off my time, couldn't I?)

My longest training run had been 18 miles, and it was at this point in the race that I began to feel like a poor swimmer out of his depth. For the first time I walked at a drinks station, then trundled forward again. Then I slowed for another walk, ran, then walked again. Up to this point I had been running well, but I was now jogging along in a flat, stubbing gait, which caused my toes to press at each step against the front of my shoe. I was aware of this but powerless to do anything about it. Although my ability to do mental arithmetic had (as always during a run) forsaken me, I had been aware for the last few miles that I was going to be much slower than my target time. The last mile was, however, enjoyable because of the terrific support from the crowd. For me—a person who has never earned much applause as a runner—this was a wonderful novelty. Tired though I was, I managed to wave as enthusiastically to the spectators as they did to us.

Crossing the finish line brought the huge physical relief, and any disappointment over the time was lost in the elation of finishing the most famous marathon race in the world. The arrangements for dealing with 36,000 exhausted runners were very good, and I picked up another bulging goody bag and went to meet Pat, Fiona and her friend Elizabeth, with whom we had run in Paris a few years earlier. There was a handsome medal and an interesting selection of goodies in the bag, but I was disappointed with the finisher's T-shirt, which had an over-the-top statement: "You see impossible, I saw the finish line." I've never worn it since.

Both big toes suffered, and I lost the nail on the right one after it had gone through all the colours of the rainbow. Other than that I came away from the event intact, no abrasions worth speaking about, and—apart from a couple of cramping twinges—no muscle tiredness at all. My expert but callous children attribute this lack of suffering to not having tried hard enough. Maybe they are right. The water and dextrose drink provision was very good, and I would say that it is not necessary for runners of my modest ability to take in water before the start; it only increases the need for toilet stops during the race.

So, job done! The record shows that I was 12978th overall, 208th in my age group with a time of 4 hrs 31 mins and 06 secs. I experienced elation, of course, but this emotion struggled to dominate tiredness, and so after a shower I opted for a pot of tea rather than anything more traditional at a celebration. All round the hotel were groups with at least one red-faced, bemedalled finisher. We nodded respectfully at each other.

As the family returned to Scotland the next day I had more questions than answers in my head:

Why did I have to walk towards the end? Was the warmth of the weather to blame? What time might I have made if I had kept on running all the way? Should I have put in a longer training run?

These questions will haunt me until I have had another bash at this distance...

Daft as a Brush

David

WHILE WORKING IN EDINBURGH, I had a mid-week day off. It was mid-June and an area of high pressure had settled over Central Scotland; fine weather was forecast for the next few days. I devised a plan to run the Ben Lui Horseshoe. I left Edinburgh at midnight before my free day and drove over empty roads up to Crianlarich. Shortly afterwards I turned off the A82, up the old gold mine road, parked up near Cononish and rested. Only some ticking noises from the cooling engine disturbed the silence, and soon I fell asleep. At first light the clear, windless conditions had me up, raring to go. But first, to decide what to wear and carry! I opted for a peaked cap, T-shirt and shorts, with white ankle socks and running shoes. Round my waist I had a skier's bum bag, containing water, energy bars, small map section, compass, space blanket, lip salve and bandages. Attached to the waist strap were a towel and a cagoule. A last swig of water and a couple of energy bars, and I was off.

The path to Beinn Dubhchraig wound its way through birch trees and bracken, dry and crusty from the baking sun of the previous days. The birds were in full voice, and I settled into a busy, rhythmic pace which soon had me emerging onto a wide summit ridge. I approached the summit well before 7 a.m., but to my surprise, I saw a group of climbers already there. They were all studying maps, and, I guess, were on a course and had spent the night nearby. From the feet up they were in full climbing gear—heavy boots and gaiters, over-trousers, Goretex anoraks and woolly hats, with large rucksacks on their backs, two trekking poles each. Intent on their map-reading, they were unaware of my approach until I was quite close. One turned and looked at me, then invited the others to look at me. They all turned and gazed at me. I was a red-faced, chubby 60-year old dressed as for a 10km road race. I distinctly heard one of them mutter: "Daft as a brush!" I nodded a greeting, then stopped at the cairn and drank some water. They continued to pore over their maps and ignored me, and I them.

After a minute or so I turned back down my path towards Ben Oss, an easy jog with beautiful scenery to admire on all sides. From that peak I skirted the wide, southern slopes of Ben Lui and slogged my way along the broad rump between Lui and Beinn a' Chleibh, an uninspiring dome which nevertheless had excellent views down Glen Lochy and beyond to Ben Cruachan. I reached the cairn at 10 a.m.; it was becoming much warmer now, and a heat haze masked the outline of Ben Lui as I retraced my route north-east. I had to slow down to a careful walk for the rocky cap to the hill, where I stopped to admire wonderful views in all directions. I opted for the gully descent into the corrie and picked my way slowly down the faint path over steep rock and scree. One or two walkers panting their way uphill looked at me with curiosity—perhaps respectful in recognition of my early start, or perhaps disdainful of my light clothing and cavalier approach to the hills. Once back on more gently-sloping terrain near Allt an Rund I reverted to a good running pace and reached my car by noon. I had completed the horseshoe in quick time in ideal conditions, and reached home at 4 p.m.

This took place eleven years ago. The day stands out from many runs and many hill days as memorable because of that overheard comment: "Daft as a brush!" I liked it, and, as I ran repeated it with a chuckle, over and over. I had reacted to the weather conditions by taking minimal gear, and so enjoyed a 5-star mountain run in a beautiful group of hills. Maybe brushes aren't so daft after all!

How to Buy a Sofa

David

"QUITE A LOT OF FLIES around here," I chirped to my wife as I bent to the ground from the driver's seat to tie my trail shoe laces.

On Friday evening we had planned this Saturday morning amicably over a glass or two of wine. I wanted to go for a long run, and she wanted to look at sofas. We decided that the best place for sofas was 30 miles away in Tillicoultry. She would drop me off 9 miles away in Glendevon then drive to the warehouse and inspect the sofas. I would run over the hills, freshen up in the warehouse toilets, then we would try to agree over the choice of sofa.

I waved to the departing car, took a deep breath, then set off up the track, which runs up the southern flank of Glensherrup Reservoir. Yes, there were quite a few flies. They were large black flies, and they acted as if I were the best thing that had happened to them for some time. They buzzed above my head excitedly, taking turns to land on my bare arms, head and legs. Their excitement was infectious, and soon they formed a fast-moving cloud above my head. I had with me a sweat rag, which I waved and flapped in an effort to shoo them away—to no effect. The track rose steeply up the side of a belt of conifers and I was soon sweating freely, which seemed to attract more flies. I gave up with my sweat rag and picked up a long, bushy branch. I swished it round my head and it did bring some relief. Unfortunately the rotary movement slowed down my running, which allowed the flies to adopt a holding pattern just out of range of the branch. Inevitably my arm tired and down they swooped! In my frustration I wondered: Are these flies the same ones I noticed down by the road, or have they stayed in their territory and passed me on to their mates? Have they got it in for me? Why?

I usually breathe through the mouth when I run, so—and I suppose it was inevitable—I swallowed one. In years of jogging this has happened to me more than once, and it remains one of my most unpleasant experiences. No amount of spitting could bring up this little fellow, and he fluttered and kicked his way down into my body. (A shiver passes through my body just from writing this...) Swallowing the fly turned my mood from annoyed to desperate. How could I escape this torture? Is there any bog myrtle—it is reputed to keep midges at bay. As the head is most attractive to them, could I make a hat out of heather or ferns? If I met anyone with insect repellent, could I flog them my watch in exchange for a good squirt? Will I find a stiff breeze at the top to blow the wee blighters away? I reached the end of the wood and ran over level, open ground. Sadly there was not a breath of wind. I was, however, able to run faster, and my planned easy jog to Tillicoultry became a frantic scurry. The flies kept pace. Shouting at them didn't help, and shouting wasn't easy, either, because of the heavy panting. I was at my wits' end.

Ahead of me and slightly off to the right I spotted two people who were standing still, consulting their map. Immediately I altered course and sped up to them. I was wide-eyed, damp and covered in pine needles, crimson-faced. My chest was heaving and I felt like a fugitive from a battlefield. They looked at me curiously as I blurted out: "Could you just confirm exactly where we are, please?" I moved in close and peered at their map. A finger pointed silently to our location. "Thanks," I muttered, then ducked low and sped off towards Maddy Moss and Tillicoultry. It worked!

The flies were tricked and missed my cunning move. They stayed with their new friends! Unescorted I reached the lip of the plateau and started down the steep path to the town. The lack of buzzing flies was pure joy! For the first time I was able to enjoy the run and the views, and felt almost human again by the time I reached the warehouse.

I was towed round the aisles of the warehouse to the sofa selected by my wife as most suitable. I sat on it, meekly accepted it and queued blissfully to do the paperwork. Sign here? No problem. Thank you very much. Delivery in 6 weeks? Whatever! My wife looked at me curiously, but said nothing. She had the sofa she wanted, and I was aglow with the memory of my battle with the flies and eventual victory. All in all it had been a good day out for both of us.

In Amongst the Trophies

David

WHEN I AM AT HOME I always run on Sunday mornings. The club meets at 10 a.m., and I can usually find some runners of my standard for a decent hour's run round the local area. When I am away from home I become restless as Sunday approaches, and try to make sure I can keep up the habit of a good leg-stretch before Sunday lunch.

On the last Sunday in March I was in St Keverne, Cornwall, where the rain was slightly warmer than back home in Scotland. Earlier in the week I had had a run along part of the Cornish Coastal Footpath, but the muddy conditions and high wind had made this hard work. It looked as though I would have a run round the country lanes on Sunday, until I spotted in my running magazine that there was a race nearby in Helston that day called An-Resek Hellys 10, "undulating terrain, changing facilities, entry on the day, 10.30 a.m. start." I decided to enter, feeling that 10km would allow me to slip away for not much more than an hour and a half, then rejoin my family. The rain had moderated to a steady drizzle, there was no wind, and I looked forward to the run.

I now know that 10 means 10 miles, not 10km, so at the start I had to swallow hard, as 10 miles would take me—in my state of training at that time—out of my comfort zone.

As we lined up at the start I introduced myself to the marshal wearing a "Last Runner" bib and told him that we might get to know one another better over the race. He told me that half of the field had done this! I placed myself at the rear of the field and started gently. If it had been a 10km race I would have settled for a time of 55-60 minutes, so I tried to project a time for the longer distance. One hour 40 minutes with a fair wind...

The first few hundred metres were uphill on a road, then the course led gently downhill through shops to a riverside park. Nearly all the other runners wore Cornish running club vests; they were all shapes and sizes, all ages. I asked one chap of my age, running at my pace, if he had run the race before. He said he had run it several times, his best time being 99 minutes. "No chance of that this year," he went on, "too wet and muddy." I had thought of latching on to someone like him, but after a couple of minutes I found that I wanted to drive on. As the stony path wound round the hillside I threaded my way through slower runners, sometimes enjoying a short chat, sometimes nipping silently through. I noted the mile markers with a feeling of growing delight. I was feeling good and enjoying this race!

The route left the track at Mile 4 and descended steeply to the beach. It could only have been 400 metres, but the crossing of a soft sand spit took the steam out of all of us. Once back on more solid ground I found that I had caught up with a long snake of runners trying to negotiate a steep narrow climb on churned-up mud. Hedges with brambles lined the path, so it was not easy to find a dry line of grass without ripping skin and clothes on the thorns. Now I don't mind dirty shoes, so I charged up the middle of the path while more fussy runners were picking their way round the worst bits. It was tiring, but once again I was picking off quite a few runners. Soon we reached a narrow road, which made its way uphill to the main road at the Naval Air Base of Culdrose. To my amazement I still had some energy left, and kept up a decent pace until the Finish. I crossed the line at 94 minutes by my watch, so was pleased with that.

We returned to Scotland on Monday. There was a message on my answer-phone saying that I had come 3rd in my age group, and did I want to collect my trophy or have it sent to my home. Trophy??? For readers who don't know me, I am not your trophy-winning runner, more the plodding old bloke at the back. I am happy to take part in an event and get the T-shirt. Running trophy?? *Moi*?? I checked the race details on the website. This race offers trophies to 1st, 2nd and 3rd place runners in 8 male and 7 female age groups! "Send it up!" I replied, "Send it up, please!"

Later that week the full results were published, so I (trophy-winner) scanned them eagerly. There I was, timed at 1hr 34 mins 30 secs, and 284th out of 393. Not bad! I just checked to see how others in my age group had done. 1st and 2nd were two locals who were quite close to each other at 1hr 17 and 1hr 19. Possibly an old rivalry? Then there was a long gap until my own name at 1 hr 34, and then—nothing! In my age group there were three runners, and I came last.

My trophy will be prominently displayed at home. If anyone admires it, I think I will keep some of the less important details of the race as my little secret.

Hail, Runner on the Bridge!

David

I OFTEN WORK AWAY from home, and drive the length and breadth of Britain. It's no longer a novelty, more a matter of routine when I haul the suitcase out of the cupboard and pack for my trip. The running kit goes into the case before anything else; a top, shorts and socks—perhaps a cap, gloves and a cagoule in cold weather. Wherever I am, however taxing my schedule, I always find time to go for a run. As I lay the kit in the case, I wonder what form my runs will take. Rural, or built-up? Alone, or will I find another runner? I finish packing, put the case in the boot and set off.

So, here I am, driving down a motorway to my destination, numb in bum and bored with driving, and every now and then I pass under a bridge. I look up warily, checking for small boys with an attitude and some stones, and also looking out for The Runner on the Bridge.

I can't believe the number of times I see a lone runner—perhaps in lime green top, black tracksuit trousers and black hat—crossing a bridge above me at a purposeful loping stride, eyes looking straight ahead.

I watch the runner as long as I can, thinking: "Go on, mate! Enjoy! I'll be doing the same in a few hours."

That really lifts the spirits!

A Fleeting Memory

David

I DROVE PAST Fleet Services in Hampshire the other day and the memory of a run I did there three or four years ago flashed vividly across my brain.

My wife and I spent a night there on the way to some event. Early the next day I put on my running kit, came out of the hotel on the southbound side of the M3 and surveyed my options. It was 6 a.m. on a summer morning, the weather was clear and fresh after rain and, with my wife still fast asleep and in no hurry to take breakfast, I had no time pressure. I chose to go right and jogged down the exit road to the south. A pleasant smell came from tall pines, and the wet road glistened in the sunlight. I soon reached a T-junction and it was decision time again. This time my decision had implications; going left would take me through a new-ish housing estate. It would not be too difficult to make a loop along suburban streets and cycle paths and return to the Services from the north. Turning right would take me under the motorway and into the unknown. Of course I went right. The awareness that you have to find a safe and legal way to cross a railway line, canal, river or motorway adds a little spice to a run!

Once I had crossed under the motorway I found myself in open country, and settled into a steady running pace. I stayed on the roadside pavement for several minutes until it finished at a junction and did not restart at the far side. Taking this as a sign I turned right into a narrow lane with high hawthorn hedges which climbed steadily upwards. Looking ahead I could see the grassy crest of a hill, so plodded on for the challenge of the ascent and potential of good views. Indeed there were good views, and an inviting stile led to a footpath roughly parallel to the motorway far below me. I ran carefully through fields of grazing cows and sheep, and relaxed to enjoy the fruits of my hill-climbing labour. Perhaps I relaxed too much, because I lost the line of the path and found myself running along the fence dividing two fields, but with no obvious path exit anywhere. No problem, I thought, I've done enough. I'll just work my way down to the motorway then run along until I find a crossing possibility.

The first part was eventful; to leave my field I had to ease my way through a gap in the straggly hedge, which was reinforced by blackberry thickets. It was a delicate operation, but as I stepped into the next field I noticed a gate low on the right. The plan was working... Beyond the gate was another field, this time with a tractor track leading nicely in my desired direction. I followed it to a road and began to stride out on a pleasant down gradient, when the road turned sharply to the left and started to climb uphill. Going uphill again was not on my agenda! I turned and ran back along the road until I reached a narrow straggly wood of mixed trees which offered a possible route home. To begin with all went well; the trees were well-spaced, and there were clearings with pheasant feeding canisters and well-worn animal paths.

I made good progress, and started thinking about the breakfast I was earning with this effort, when I came to the sting in the tail. Firstly the well-spaced trees became dense bushes and I was forced to walk, then I met the first ancient barbed-wire fence, deep in the wood and supported by rotting posts. The last obstacle was a swamp, which I managed to squeeze round by side-stepping along a continuation of the old wire fence. The motorway was close at this stage; I could hear the roar of heavy vehicles passing above me. Sure enough I came to an embankment guarded by a 2-meter wide ditch of slow-moving, dark, oily water. Should I go left or right? I knew that there were Services on the northbound side of the motorway, but in which direction? Comparing roughly how far I had run before and after crossing under the motorway, I reckoned that I was to the north, so turned right and made my way along the bank of the ditch. By this stage I was anxious. The euphoria of the early stage of the run had vanished. While there were signs of human activity where I was, they were not of recent years. It was dank and mouldy and spattered with litter thrown or blown from the road above. I moved carefully along the narrow gap between ditch and impenetrable woodland. I had to concentrate, and so it was some time before I realised that traffic noise had subsided to an occasional gentle humming. Concluding that I had now reached the place where the bank led up to the Services and not the road, I decided to cross the ditch. I found a clean branch and probed the water. The branch sank alarmingly deep into the murky liquid. Breakfast seemed a long way away.... A glimmer of hope came when I spotted a pipe crossing the ditch. Although the pipe was too slender to be used as a bridge, it had square concrete supports on either bank which could double as take-off and landing sites.

After a risk assessment heavily influenced by hunger and desperation I launched myself from one concrete pillar to the other, and almost made it.... My leading leg was fine, but the trailing one pulled me relentlessly backwards. When my body came to rest I was half in and half out of the water, embracing the pillar tightly. Whew!

When my heart rate had slowed down enough, I slid down the pillar until my feet stuck fast in the chilly mud. The drama was over—all that was left was the embarrassment. I struggled up the embankment and picked my way through vast quantities of litter to the Services perimeter, which was interwoven fencing. This was an easy obstacle to cross thanks to a strong tree with a branch overhanging the car-park on the other side. Soon I was mingling with people (the first I had seen since I had left from the Services over an hour ago!) and heading for the pedestrian bridge which crosses the road. My decision to jog this crossing was not for the sake of the exercise, it was to minimise the time people could gaze at me—soaked from the waist down in noisome liquid, filthy and scratched as I was. Unfortunately the squelching of my trainers drew attention to me, so curious eyes followed my dripping progress.

Showered, dressed, breakfasted, and checked out from the hotel, we drove on south. I can remember the run very clearly, but for the last month or so neither my wife nor I have been unable to remember what event it was that brought us to spend the night in Fleet Services in the first place!

A Friend in Need

David

I WAS WORKING AT RAF SCAMPTON, just north of Lincoln, as a member of an Arms Control team. To the east of the camp the flat farmlands stretched into the far distance, and to the west the ground dipped steeply down into the Till Valley. A few of us went running in our free time; public footpaths criss-crossed the fields, and we could easily avoid the busy A15 and A1500 roads. What we could not avoid was the cold wind, and my lasting memory of those runs is the buffeting gales which swept over the tree-less terrain.

One weekend I chickened out of the stressful drives home to Scotland and back. At coffee break on Friday I found out from my friend Pete, who lived locally, that the Lincoln 10km race took place that Sunday. Both he and his wife Judith were planning to run. I had run many a mile with this couple, and decided I would have a go. "Register early," said Pete, "it is very popular."

I joined a long queue to register, and completed the business with over an hour to spare. Fortunately I had parked nearby, so sat in the car with the paper until it was time for the warm-up. As always, the other runners looked to me to be younger, fitter, faster—and there were masses of them! I saw no sign of Pete and Judith.

The race started and I made the usual mistake of setting off too quickly. After 6km I was flagging, and then hit the barrier of pain and self-pity. I struggled on, then Judith overtook me! She did not see me, and was loping along with an easy stride. I felt an immediate surge of positive energy, and my own stride became more relaxed and comfortable. She had gained 50m on me, but I made no attempt to catch up; instead, I kept up Judith's pace and held her blonde hair and black T-shirt in view.

At the 9km marker I found I was catching up with her, although my pace had not altered. I peered ahead and could see that Judith was slowing down, hands on hips and the rhythm gone. I realised that I would draw level shortly, and thought about what I should do. Should I encourage her? "Not long now, Judith! Keep going! You can do it!" Should I drop down to her speed to support and cross the line with her? Should I leave her in her personal distress?

When I was 10m behind her she veered to the left of the road and dropped down to a walk. I decided not to make contact and sailed past on the right, eyes straight ahead. I crossed the line, collected the goody bag, then turned back to watch Judith finish. I waited for several minutes but did not see her, or Pete, for that matter. Disappointed, I made my way home.

On Monday morning I sought out Pete to find out how he and Judith had enjoyed the race. He looked at me in surprise, then explained that they had left it too late and had not been able to register! They had gone shopping.

Now I would like to contact a black T-shirted, blonde lady runner in the Lincoln 10km who was heading for a time of 50 minutes or so, but who faded dramatically near the finish. I'd like to thank her for the lift.

EUROPE

And Yet...

David

IN 2007 WE PICKED LISBON for our family marathon experience; a city we didn't know, still warm enough in early December and with enough culture for the family non-runner. We entered three runners for the Full and one for the Half Marathon, booked rooms, rental car and flights on-line and started the pre-race training.

Heavy rain fell as we drove from the airport, and Lisbon showed us a dour face. On our first evening we ate in a restaurant near our hotel, where a football match between Benfica and Man United was being screened. The diners were quietly indifferent to the game; only the waiting staff gave it their full attention, so we had "extra time" over the meal. The next morning we set off to register. This was no easy task, as there were no signs at the discreet door of the municipal building where a temporary office had been established. The staff treated us with a cool, distant politeness, as if we were seeking planning permission for a garden shed. Lack of the usual lycra-clad bustle at registration gave a surreal atmosphere. When we asked if there was a runners' market the reply was a dismissive shrug. Our only hope for that tingle of anticipation when you meet other runners would be the pasta party on the eve of the race.

We took the city "hop on – hop off" bus tour, dodging the wind and showers, and learned something of the Portuguese nation and its tradition of maritime exploration, and even managed a short training run before the pasta party. If we had hoped for that pre-race tingle at the party, we were very disappointed! A hundred or so of us queued in respectful silence on a staircase of a hotel, until a door was thrown open to reveal a Victorian soup kitchen, offering spaghetti with tomato sauce, a piece of fruit and bottled water. Each ticket was for a half-hour slot. "Eat your pasta then go— someone else needs your seat." No speech of welcome, no music, nothing. A Portuguese runner we spoke to was scathing in his criticism, and told us that we would be better running the marathon in Oporto. He was from Oporto. We went to bed in sombre mood. Lisbon had hardly welcomed us runners with open arms.

It was the morning of the race, and the rain had steadied to a constant drizzle. We set off early to secure a good parking space near the square where the Start and Finish would be. There was no problem finding a space, because nothing was happening! Members of a brass band sheltered in doorways, and some workers put out some crowd barriers, and that was it! There were four portaloos on the square, one of which was not working, and we wondered if we had come on the wrong day, or to the wrong place.

We knew that the Full marathon runners were to start 90 minutes before the Half field. Their route was A to B and back, A to C and back, A to D and back, then A almost to B and back. (This was good news for our non-runner, who saw us passing lots of times!) Half runners ran the second half of the full course, and had to deduct 21km from each marker to monitor their progress. The course was mainly flat, with a dull, industrial area in one direction but wide boulevards with flower beds along the wide River Tejo in the other. The three working portaloos at the Start remained the only concession for a call of nature for 5,000 runners! Puddles were a nuisance, also pedestrians with umbrellas who walked arm-in-arm and studiously ignored runners. There were very few enthusiastic spectators. I did the Half, and enjoyed waving at my son, daughter-in-law and daughter, who all did the Full marathon, as we criss-crossed on several occasions. The wet conditions kept runners cool, and I splashed along at a steady clip, but I had little idea of my progress in the race, and the same held for any other Brit Half runners I chatted to en route.

There was—I admit—something of an atmosphere at the Finish. The band played, and a man with a frenzied voice and a microphone competed with it. An official separated Full and Half runners by the colour of their start numbers and we queued to receive our medals and bags—the Full medal appropriately larger than the Half one. Most of the spectators were supporters of individual runners; Lisbon went about its normal business on a wet Sunday morning. We gathered at the car, returned to our hotel for a shower and meal, agreeing that it had been the worst-organised marathon of our experience...

And yet...

Romana, our first-time marathon runner had completed ahead of expectations, the other two Full runners had achieved PBs, and my Half was faster than anticipated. As the years roll on, this will be the abiding memory: a good time was done by all.

The Forerunner

David

THERE WAS NO MOVEMENT or noise at the Start, as I tightened the laces of my running shoes and shouldered my daysack. It was, after all, 6 a.m., still 4 hours before the start of the race.

I jogged through the Start gate in solitude, and headed along the track which climbed into the dense woods. I could imagine the pack of runners four hours later, a patter of footfalls and a whiff of embrocation as 180 athletes tackled the course, my son Andrew amongst them. This was Garmisch Partenkirchen, and the day of the annual Osterfelder Mountain Race, 11.5km with 1033m height to be gained; not for the faint-hearted. I was pleased to note that the route markers were easily seen and plentiful—blue and white Asics-marked plastic strips tied to trees or held on the ground by stones. Good!

The track was wide and firm underfoot, despite the recent heavy rain. It climbed in gentle curves, but the markers soon pointed to a detour, as there was a blockage on the track ahead. I turned off the track onto a narrow, soggy path through the dripping trees, and I imagined the runners here—shoving, elbowing, cursing. I crossed an open field, which in winter is a ski piste, where I could imagine impatient runners overtaking with relief after the narrow path, but I thought: Steady! There's still a long way to go.

I rejoined the track above the blockage and progressed at a gentle jog up to the Tonihütte, the first waymarker on the route. Four km behind me and 400m gained—so far, so good. The Tonihütte was still silent, but hopefully had summer guests sleeping inside, who would later enjoy the open air pool and sports facilities. The plastic markers took me onto a narrow path which started level but soon led up a steep slope in a series of switchbacks. The low cloud had patches of blue sky and it was gratifying to look down at the sleepy town of Garmisch, already far below. Admiring the scenery meant slowing down, however, as I had to be wary of tree roots, stones and steps on the path floor. Overtaking would be difficult here; perhaps gaining a few places on the open ski slope below would have been worthwhile after all? Soon I reached another ski piste, where improvement work was ongoing. Vehicles had churned up the soft ground, and for the next 200-300m it was like crossing a steep ploughed field. This will sort out the field, I thought.

The next waymarker is the Tröglhütte, at the junction of major ski pistes. Another steep, narrow path led me puffing up to the Kreuzeck Ridge—7.5km covered and 750m climbed. Along the ridge was a pleasant level trot, even downhill briefly, and with short glimpses of the magnificent view into the wooded Partnach Valley. Looking ahead I saw a dark grey building high above me, and recognised it as the Osterfelder cable car station where the race finishes. I thought that this view would either horrify or spur on the runners, depending on how much fuel they had left in their tanks. It was still a wind-free morning but low cloud obscured the rocky triangle of the Alpspitze which towers above this stretch of the course. I branched left towards the sleepy Hochalm restaurant, where the prize-giving would take place in the afternoon, knowing that I was now on the last leg of the race course. Although the route was now along a broad track again, there was a sting in the tail, as there were two steep parts ahead. Start your final sprint too soon, and you'll regret it! I followed the track through a hole blasted through the rock and saw the Osterfelder a short distance above me. For me the empty terrace signalled the end of my lone ascent, which had started out as a run but had degenerated to a purposeful walk in places. For the runners later on it represented The Finish—achievement, refreshment, comradeship and, for some, the glory of victory in their age category.

I reached the terrace and was spotted by the caretaker, who offered me the use of his shower, and a welcome cup of coffee. By 9.30 a.m. I was in clean clothes, with a good Bavarian breakfast inside me, and ready for the race, surely the most eager spectator of the day! I had thoroughly enjoyed following the trail of markers up the mountain. It had given me the flavour of the event without the fever of competition. I had had time to pick my way over difficult terrain, appreciate the scenery and drink in the peace of the early morning mountain. Being a fore-runner was as good as taking part in the race; I must try to do this again!

Gel Hell

Fiona

I **ARRIVED IN PRAGUE** fit, well prepared, injury-free and excited to run my 11th marathon. A minor hiccup by BA losing my bag in transit meant I nearly had to buy new trainers the day before the event but thankfully my worn-in, comfortable shoes arrived in the nick of time. I had chosen my clothes carefully for the race taking the weather forecast into account, had my start number all pinned on to my top and had studied the route carefully, memorising various landmarks and places of interest to look out for, etc. I was ready! All that had to be done now was to load up some carbohydrates at the pasta party and get an early night. While enjoying my macaroni and taking in the entertainment that was laid on for us I noticed a man going around dishing out promotional sachets of energy gel. Not wanting to miss out on a freebie, I took a handful of these gels and stuffed them in my pocket.

Race day arrived and after a good night's sleep I was itching to get on with it. I followed my usual routine of an early breakfast and a strong coffee before getting dressed for the race and heading to the start in plenty of time to soak up the atmosphere and do a decent warm up jog. The weather was just as forecast, fresh but dry with a light breeze, so I was dressed perfectly and raring to go. Just before leaving the hotel room I spotted the sachets of energy gel on the bedside table and picked them up. It's worth saying at this point that I had never tried one of these energy sachets before, neither had I ever run with one. By the time I got to the starting area I was already fed up with carrying them in my hand and wondered what else I should do with them. Just then I saw someone wearing a very sophisticated looking belt with sachets, drink shots and energy bars all strategically placed around his middle which gave me the idea of just securing the sachets in the waist band of my shorts which I duly did and felt comfortable with the arrangement. At this point I decided I would take the first sachet at mile 15 and, if needed, the second at about mile 22 to carry me over the finish line in good form. Strategy all worked out, I was confident and excited about the race ahead and started to imagine PBs and sprint finishes with the help of my newfound secret weapon.

The gun fired and we were off, but soon after mile one I lost one of the sachets down my shorts and had a very awkward few moments of digging around to retrieve it and then tying the drawstring on my shorts tighter than I would normally find comfortable to ensure it didn't happen again. A few miles passed without incident before I began to feel the chafing of these foil sachets against my skin so I knew I needed to find a new home for them. The next place I tried was down my socks, one on each foot and this felt great, in fact I could hardly feel they were there. That was until they worked their way up and, indeed, out of my sock. One was lost but I managed to grab the other one just before it escaped for good. Its third resting place was under the strap of my bra/running top just under my shoulder. Finally I felt I had found a good place for it and could concentrate on the race and the next 6 miles before the 15 mile mark which was the appointed gel-taking marker. As I passed the 22km mark (approx 14 miles) I took the sachet out and looked to see how to open it and eat it while on the run. There was a little mark saying "tear here" so I tore the top off the sachet as instructed and the contents immediately spewed out all over my hand. I should say at this point that the flavour of the energy gel was apple crumble, so not only was the liquid sticky and gooey but it also had lumps of crumble in it. Yuk! With very sticky hands and goo all over the sachet I tried to actually get some of it in my mouth—easier said than done when you're running a race. I did succeed in consuming some of it but not without getting a fair amount of it over my lips and chin. I was now in a real mess with hands so sticky I couldn't drop the sachet and had to run along desperately trying to flick the thing out of my gooey fingers. Finally I was rid of the blasted thing and could concentrate on trying to tidy myself up and lose the horrible sweet, sickly taste in my mouth. Thankfully I saw a sign saying "Refreshments in 1km" so knew it would only be another 5 or 6 minutes before I could wash myself down with a bottle of water and get on with running the race and achieving a personal best time. However, to my horror the refreshment on offer was a sweet, sickly energy drink—in a cup! Better than nothing, I tried to wash my hands in orange lucozade, but in pouring it onto my hands from the cup I ended up with it all down my legs so the problem now was not contained to hands and mouth but was really a full body issue!

Finally after another 3km I got the bottle of water I was longing for and was able to wash my hands, face and legs and enjoy the last section of the race in relative comfort.

Sadly, I didn't get the PB I was hoping for and didn't finish the race in the sprightly form I was imagining, but the distraction of the apple crumble at the halfway point did prevent me from hitting 'the wall' so there is a small positive to come out of it.

The moral of this story is not to avoid energy gel sachets at all costs (although I have to say I haven't tried one since!) but it is to always test things out during training runs and not to try something new on an event you've trained hard for, as you never know what mess you might find yourself in!

Friendship Between Runners

David

IT WAS ROUND ABOUT the halfway point on the Paris Marathon that the little lady elbowed me. She was "of a certain age," trim of figure and immaculately dressed with a white band round her short hair, gold earrings and a white running outfit which could have been designed exclusively for her. I always run on the right for some reason, and was quite close to a wall when Madame pushed past me. The reason for her to be hugging the right-hand side of the route was that she had a small white dog on a lead to her right. The dog was equally trim, and was even wearing a start number! She drew away from me, but I was curious and kept her in view. Both she and the dog were very light on their feet and they were trotting along rhythmically. Madame ran with a rapid, efficient motion which hinted at many hours of pre-race training. The dog showed no interest in the forest of legs or in any interesting scents along the way, it appeared to be focussed only on the Finish. Several times I saw Madame elbow aside another unwary runner, and on went the pair of them.

At a drinks station I caught up with them; the dog was enjoying a bowl of water (where did the bowl come from?) and Madame was watching intently. My curiosity was now mixed with distaste, as I considered the wee dog to be a potential hazard, and I think she caught my disdainful look as I lumbered past.

I had forgotten about them over the next few minutes, and was chatting to a fellow runner when I felt the dig in the back, and the pair of them overtook me with gentle ease. Again I watched as they threaded their way past runners like me on the extreme right; a push here, an extended hand there; I didn't hear a sound from Madame or dog. This time I kept up with them, and, with every push, or if I spotted a near accident with the lead, I became more indignant. What stupidity to bring a dog when there are so many runners! When they stopped at the next drinks station I gave Madame as withering a look as I could muster as I passed.

For the weaker runner like me there is a horrible point near the end of the route when you turn into a park and swing left. In front of you is a stream of runners going right, and going fast because they are near the Finish. We who are turning left know that we are running away from that wonderful place where we cross the line. I was suffering at this point, when Madame and dog ran slowly past me in the same trotting action, both with eyes fixed straight ahead. I groaned out loud in exasperation. Dogs in parks, yes, but dogs in a marathon, no, definitely no! I converted my annoyance into adrenalin, and gave chase. Now my target was not the Finish, it was the Finish before the hated pair! I concentrated on their backs and dug in. It was made slightly easier for me because they had to weave in and out of people walking, which I could do more efficiently. I saw the hand-off and the push, but I am convinced that Madame uttered no sound. Such arrogance! Beneath her to talk to fellow runners, eh? With a huge effort I overtook them on the right, but it was my turn to ignore them and keep the eyes focussed ahead.   Jubilant, I concentrated on keeping the pace and there would be no chance of them keeping up with me.

With 300m to go we rounded a square and it was nearly all over. Fortuitously the crowd of runners thinned out, and I glanced across to see Madame on the extreme left, the lead in her left hand and the dog by her left side! What's more, their six little legs were going very, very fast! I tried, oh how I tried, to catch them but they crossed the line some 4 or 5 places ahead of me. I collected my goodies bag and medal and slumped onto the ground in a quiet corner, some 50-60m away from the Finish. My head went down and I just sat there, gathering my strength for the walk back to the hotel and that bath. Suddenly I felt a tap on my shoulder. Madame was leaning down with a white polystyrene cup of hot, sweet tea in her outstretched hand. She acknowledged my thanks with a short nod, and was off.

What a charming fellow-runner! Such a gracious lady, and how nice that she brought her dog with her for the race!

The Grossglockner Experience

Andrew

IT **WAS ONE OF THOSE** crack-of-the-morning starts that actually felt more like getting up in the middle of the night. The plan was for me to take the 6.30 a.m. train to Krun where my Russian friend Sergei would pick me up, then drive to Heiligenblut in Austria for the Grossglockner mountain race. The first part of the journey went well. I cycled to the train station, caught the train and there was Sergei waiting for me at Krun.

The race didn't start until 11 a.m., but I knew it was a long way and I was eager to get going. Sergei was very relaxed about the driving and insisted on going first to his place for a cup of tea. To our surprise his Mum and Dad, who were visiting him at the time, were up; they decided to come along as well. Sergei tried to persuade his Mum not to come as he knew she was prone to car sickness, but she was fixed on the idea and that was that.

So it was considerably later than planned that we finally set off. The weather was excellent and the scenery breathtaking as we passed Achensee, through Zillertal then up the Gerlos Pass. Sergei's Mum and Dad, who had divorced many years before, were deep in a rather heated Russian conversation for most of the journey. At one point I asked Sergei if the Russian language always sounds so aggressive or if they were really having an argument and he confirmed my fears, saying that they were having a real go at each other. At the top of the Gerlos Pass we had a quick stop to stretch the legs and Sergei took the opportunity to ask the guy at the toll booth how long from here to Heiligenblut. The man thought for a second then said about one and a half hours, at which point Sergei and I simultaneously looked at our watches—9.35 a.m.! We quickly bundled the photograph-taking parents into the car and sped off.

We reached Zell am See in good time, after which it was a long slog up the Grossglockner Pass. This road is known as one of the most beautiful and dramatic roads in Europe as it coils its way up from 700m to 2400m but we had no time to enjoy it. Sergei was driving like a man possessed. Overtaking at every half opportunity, we went screeching up the pass. I was trying to eat a banana and drink some water but ended up spilling more than I drank. Sergei's Mum had gone very quiet in the back and that, coupled with Sergei making anxious looks in the mirror and what sounded like words of encouragement, made me realise she was not enjoying the journey any more. We reached the summit, then had to go all the way down the other side. Each hairpin was numbered and I remember seeing we had 26 to go and it was 10.20 a.m.!

I had started to accept the fact that we would not make it, but thanks to some excellent driving and the roads being quiet, we arrived in Heiligenblut at 10.48 a.m. The next 12mins were quite chaotic. As we passed the road sign saying Heiligenblut, Sergei's Mum could not keep it in any longer. I heard her retch, then vomit. Why she hadn't opened the window I will never know. Sergei and I were too concerned with the race. He asked me to put the window down and ask a runner doing his warm up where we could collect the start numbers. I got as far as saying "Excuse me…" when the nausea got hold of me and I went through the convulsions of being sick without bringing anything up. The runner looked at me with a mixture of sympathy and disgust, then trotted off on his warm up.

Sergei didn't park: he just stopped. I leapt out of the car and started looking for the start number desk. Sergei caught me up, we collected our numbers, then ran back to the car and started to change. On top of everything else an Austrian policeman came over at this point and said: "In Germany you must have very different speeding laws." I looked at Sergei who assessed the situation. The start was in 6mins, we still had to change and put our start numbers on, his Mum was still being sick and he had to explain to her where to drive to in order to meet us at the finish. With all this in mind the policeman was well down on the list of priorities so Sergei dismissed him with a backhanded wave as if he were flicking away a wasp, hoping that the "wasp" would just go away though realising it could come back with a nasty sting! The policeman thankfully took pity on us and moved on.

We made it to the start with 2mins to spare; there was no need for a warm up after all the running around! I felt physically and mentally exhausted and realised that Sergei was probably in a worse state after all the strains of the drive—and now we were expected to run 13k, with 1200m ascent, and in a stifling heat!

The first half of the race went okay, although I found it difficult to get into a rhythm. There were long flat stretches, then it would go very steeply up, then down a bit and so on. My real problems came in the last third of the race. We had come well above the tree line and were now on the terminal moraine of the glacier when I started to get terrible stomach pain. My stomach started bubbling and gurgling and I was sure I was going to have diarrhoea. I looked around; okay, there were plenty of big rocks to hide behind but the last bit of vegetative wiping material was about 2km down the valley. To my huge relief the pain passed, so with renewed determination I picked up the pace in an attempt to catch the people who had passed me when I had had to slow due to the stomach pain. I trod on a loose stone and fell. It wasn't all that dramatic, I only grazed my hand but it gave me quite a scare.

From then on I concentrated on every step, with my head down and my eyes only on the ground a few meters ahead. I got back into my rhythm and was feeling good when a far-off cry caught my attention. I looked up a 40-meter rock face and saw some guy shouting: "The path is over here"—pointing over his shoulder. Muttering words that cannot be repeated here I launched myself at the rock-face without giving it a second thought. Three-quarters of the way up I realised what a risk I'd taken; one slip here and I'd be in serious trouble. I made it to the top and joined the path receiving a few curious looks from other runners. I thought I was about 30th but a spectator, who was counting the runners as we went by, said I was 22nd, so that gave me a lift and I managed to overtake a few more and so finished 19th. Sergei, who is better as a flat runner and cross country skier, exceeded his expectations, finishing 35th.

We met up with Sergei's parents at the finish. Mum was now much better and the journey home passed without further incident, give or take some subdued bickering in Russian in the back.

Italian Surprise

David

WE HAD NOT BOOKED, and the Youth Hostel at Garda in Northern Italy was full. The warden looked at the crestfallen faces of the four members of my family and directed us to a small hostel some 30km away at Lago di Ledro. The drive there involved a few kilometres along the shore of Lake Garda, then a white-knuckle ride on a narrow road which corkscrewed its way upwards, out of the main valley into a delightful side-valley with its own small lake amid lush green meadows flanked by the wooded foothills of the Italian Alps. The hostel had a family room for us, there was a chalet-type restaurant nearby, and the sun was shining. We booked in for four nights.

The fair weather broke on Friday, our second day. By Sunday I had had my fill of Scrabble, Connect 4 and postcard writing, but I could not persuade the family to venture outdoors. With low cloud and drizzle outside they opted to read in the dry warmth of the hostel's lounge.

I decided to set out for a run. I knew—from a walk we had done earlier—that the hilltops could be places of interest. One we had climbed still had the battlements of the Austrian defences from WWI, so I decided to run up the highest hill in the area, Cima d'Oro, in the hope of discovering another piece of history.

It was after 9 a.m. when I started, and the village was deserted. Although it was July, it was a cold, damp, still morning, and after a short climb up the forestry track I was in a misty world of my own. The track wound its way round the hill at a gentle incline, and I made good progress. After an hour or so the track and the woods ended abruptly, but a sign pointed to a narrow path and told me I would reach the summit in one hour's walking. I know that the times on these signs are an estimate for strollers, not serious walkers or joggers, so I interpreted the hour as a mere 40 minutes for me. In fact it took me much nearer the hour! The path became steep, the surface stony and I had to take care on sloping wet rock.

At last I could sense the summit as the ground levelled, and I relaxed my visual concentration on the path. At that moment my hearing sense chose to alert me. I could hear music stealing through the mist! I slowed down and peered ahead. As I reached the highest point I could make out shadowy figures—lots of them! Some were sitting on rocks, others were clustered round a central point, and most of them were dressed in sober black. From all around came singing, and from the central group, the unmistakeable sound of an accordion. There must have been over 200 people on that hilltop, and they included very young and very old. As I stood at the edge there was activity in the central group. Slowly a huge cross was raised into the vertical and secured. The singing stopped, and all bowed their heads in prayer. I had stumbled on the main part of a ceremony to dedicate the new summit cross. I watched from a respectful distance. After the ceremony the picnic hampers were opened, and I was invited to join in. Over a large cheese sandwich I learned that the old cross had been struck by lightning exactly a year ago, and that almost the entire village had come up for this ceremony, despite the miserable weather.

Elated by this totally unexpected experience I sped down the hill and proudly told the family what they had missed through fear of a little discomfort!

Kiev

David

THE CENTRE OF KIEV in winter is not a good base for someone who wants to run before or after the working day, but I was there in February and, after a hard day in the classroom, I needed my dose of adventure running. The pavements, made narrow by piles of frozen snow, were crowded and poorly lit, and the roads teemed with fuming traffic. Not far from my hotel lay a small park, however, where the paths had been cleared for recreational use. Strings of lights adorned the trees, and a kiosk at one entrance had loudspeakers which gave out cheerful music. To reach the park I had to cross the main square by subway, then pass a statue of Lenin, with arm upraised, and follow a major shopping street for two blocks.

I wove my way through the crowds to this park one evening after work, but found the paths filled with smart ladies with small dogs on long leads, some elderly walkers in tracksuits and knitted bobble hats, and a drunk. One lap round the perimeter path was probably 10-12 minutes, so I decided to do five laps. My hour of running was interesting in that it gave me a flavour of life in the city, but frustrating in that it was so repetitive. This had been merely physical exercise with pedestrian-dodging.

I ran early the next morning, well wrapped up against the sub-zero temperature. In the spirit of exploration I turned away from the route to the park, and crossed the huge main square, which was well-lit. After a few minutes I ran out of street lighting and cleared pavement, and found myself slithering on well-trodden snow and ice. With a heavy heart I returned to the square, did a few laps round it, and headed back to the warmth of my hotel.

I was free all day on Sunday, and did some sight-seeing in the morning under a sunny sky. I noticed that there were fewer people on the pavements, and much less traffic on the roads, so I took a taxi back to my hotel and put on my running gear. Setting off in a new direction I enjoyed the perfect foreign city run! My aim was a prominent group of old buildings on a distant hill—the university, I think—and I reached it and ran through graceful courtyards, cobbled alleyways and past stately buildings.

I turned for home. As the sun sank below the horizon I kept running in what I hoped was the general direction of my hotel. By sixth sense and good luck I eventually turned into a tree-lined square to see a kiosk and hear cheerful music. I had found my park! I ran a celebration lap round the perimeter path and headed back to my hotel with a feeling of satisfaction after such a varied and interesting run.

The best was yet to come, however. When I ran down the steps of the subway I could hear music—ballroom dance music. From a ghetto-blaster with a tower of speakers on a table came the warbling tones of Victor Silvester's dance band, and the entire underground concourse was filled with dancers! Elderly dancers, in overcoats and leather jackets, in headscarves and astrakhan hats, in tracksuits and in bemedalled suits, they all jostled gravely together. As many women danced with other women as with men. Non-dancers snaked their way through the dancers, ignoring them and being ignored. I was the only spectator, and I stayed for 15 minutes or so, enjoying the unexpected.

Witnessing the genteel dancing in the subway had turned a pleasant run into a memorable one!

Kill or Cure

David

STEVE AND I work together and occasionally run together at lunchtimes. He is a steady runner, whose 10km times were usually 5-6 minutes slower than mine.

We were both delighted to be asked to attend a week-long seminar in the beautiful town of Garmisch, in the south of Germany—I, because I know the place well, and Steve, because he had never been there. I told him to be sure to take his running kit.

We ran most mornings, becoming more and more adventurous as the week went on. The weather was crisp autumn at its best; cold, but sunny and clear. We would climb on trails through pine forests to look down over the Loisach Valley and up to the grey peaks: Kramer, Alpspitze and Waxenstein, the only noise being the tinkling of cowbells and distant church bells.

On our last day we were due to catch the 9.04 a.m. train back to Munich, so I planned the "Grand Finale" run, with a surprise for Steve at the end. We met as usual in the hotel lobby at 7 a.m., and started up the narrow road which winds up the grassy slopes of the Hausberg ski run. At Kochelberg-Alm we branched off left to take the steep road which climbs up the side of the Partnach Valley. We made good time, as our regular early morning excursions had accustomed us to hilly terrain. At the Partnach-Alm we admired the view over to the Wetterstein range before descending the zig-zag path down to the track junction at a wooden bridge over the river. We stopped, and I revealed my surprise. "We turn left here, and go through the Partnachklamm. The river has cut its way through the soft limestone rock for half a mile or so, forming a deep ravine, called a Klamm. We run through tunnels, and along platforms cut out of the rock, just above the river. Normally you have to pay to use this route, but at this time of the morning we should be okay."

Steve looked at me in horror. "I'm not good with tunnels," he said, "I've been claustrophobic since childhood. What are the other options?" It was then 7.45. After doing some time, speed and distance sums we both concluded that there were none. Steve gave me a withering look, then sprinted off into the dark entrance tunnel of the Klamm. I followed, taking my time to avoid puddles and low ceilings. Every now and then the tunnel opened up on the left to show the raging river, some 6 feet below. There was a continuous roar, and a mist of spray billowed up. I could see no sign of Steve ahead. I was not sure how to interpret this, but speeded up slightly. Was he okay or had his phobia literarily pushed him over the edge? There were no other people on the path—no-one to ask if a runner was ahead of me. I urged myself to run faster, but even running flat out I could not catch sight of him. At last I emerged into bright sunlight at the far end and passed through the turnstile. The place was deserted. Steve had to be ahead of me, as there were no side roads or paths, so I ran on down the narrow road alongside the now gentler stream of the Partnach. I passed the ski-jump stadium at a good pace, and was back at our hotel at 8.15. Steve's room was next to mine, and, to my great relief, I saw that his trainers were neatly placed outside his door. He must have covered the last mile and a half like a rocket! I dashed into my room to shower and pack.

I joined him in the dining room. He was sitting, red-faced and damp-haired, on his own, and, grinning sheepishly, he waved me over to join him. He apologised for not waiting, but explained that he had shot off to get through the Klamm as quickly as possible, but then thought to himself: "This is stupid! There are real risks in running pell-mell down here. I could come to harm from these real risks, just because I am spooked by irrational thoughts." He had steadied his stride and concentrated on where to put his foot down, where to duck, where to go left, where to take the right side of the walkway.

"When I came out, I felt great! In that half mile I made a huge step forward in coping with claustrophobia. Instead of waiting for you I kept on running, as I wanted time to go over in my head what I had just achieved. I do believe that I have made the breakthrough."

Steve and I caught the train with seconds to spare.

I have run with him several times since then, and he has definitely speeded up. He tells me that since Garmisch he has also made steady progress in conquering claustrophobia. This is excellent news, but we agreed that his best chance of achieving running PBs might well be if he concentrates on an event held in a tunnel, spurred on by irrational thoughts!

Mood Swings

David

I HAD LEAPT AT THE OFFER of a place at a conference in Erkelenz, in north-west Germany, but it was turning out to be a "death by power-point" experience. Even the informal seminars lacked any spark, and I was bored. All day long a warm, autumn sun had been shining, birds singing and my feet itching to go for a run. At last the day's programme was over in the conference centre, and I made my way back to my hotel, which I had chosen because it was near the edge of the town.

There was one main road bisecting our suburb, and so I planned a wide loop; left from the hotel, out into the countryside, then with left turns at every reasonable opportunity and I should strike the suburb from the other direction, rather like running a capital D, starting halfway down the vertical.

I changed quickly into my running kit and set off. Yes, it was good to be clear of the stale air of the conference centre, to be free from the lectures and noisy chat at break times, to be on my own after the crowds. There was only one thing wrong—I didn't feel right! My running had a "flat tyre" quality to it; I could hear my feet flopping onto the ground instead of rolling from heel to ball. My body felt heavy and my stomach churned. I started to explain to myself why this might be so. After that long run two days ago, perhaps still tired? A beer or three too many at the conference ice-breaker last night? A cold coming on? (There were several sneezing in my seminar group...) I ran on but decided to make this one a short run, 30-40 minutes tops; perhaps I would feel more like a longer one tomorrow? Having made my decision I plodded on, but looked for a suitable turning to bring me back to base in a straight line.

After 20 minutes I came to a peaceful village and admired its neatness as I plodded along its winding main street. Some houses still had huge sunflowers in the garden, others proudly displayed pumpkins and other harvest produce. At any turn I expected to see ahead a traffic light and road sign; I was ready for my next left turn, sure to take me back to the hotel in another 15 minutes. There was, however, no traffic light, road sign or crossroads. Looking ahead I could see vast tracts of open fields, no roads other than the one I was on. At the far end of the village was a yellow sign which told me that the next village ahead was 7km distant. I had never heard of that village and had no wish to jog 7km to explore it, so did some rapid thinking. I had been running at this point for a good half hour. I could turn round and go straight back the way I had come; low risk but a long way and boring. There had to be another way...

Erkelenz had to be somewhere on my left! Determined not to go the easy way home I went slowly back along the main street, looking for a solution. I found a paved track with a sign for cyclists leading off in the desired direction, and took it. Navigation worries had taken my mind away from my lethargy, and I found that I was running with a more positive stride. My eyes were sweeping ahead, looking for vehicles which would indicate a road and an easy way back to the hotel. There were none, but I did see what makes any runner perk up when out running—other runners, and lots of them, coming towards me! I suspect that they were members of a club on an evening meet; first, the strong runners, focussed on their performance, going hard, faces set; next the good and then the cheerful, not-so-good at the rear. The weaker ones at least gave me a smile and a friendly wave. Pride made me run as well as possible. By the time that the stragglers had passed me I was into a strong rhythm and feeling great! Pride had also prevented me from them asking directions, but I was encouraged by their presence. I managed to hold on to the improved pace and made good progress. I came to the end of the track and, sure enough, there were some 30 cars parked on the grassy edges. I had now been running for 45 minutes, and kept going straight into the town. Unsure of my whereabouts I decided to ask the first person I met for directions to Hotel Rheinischer Hof. I went over the German phrases in my mind as I ran. I had plenty of time, as the streets were deserted, and I trotted on for a further 5 minutes through suburbia. Eventually I saw a man dressed in black, leaning against a high wall and smoking. Just as I was about to open my mouth with my German question, I changed my mind and kept it shut. The man was Helmut, our barman, and the wall was the back of our hotel!

As I relaxed in my piping hot bath I reviewed my experience. After a dull day in the lecture theatre I had had high expectations for my run. The poor start was disappointing. Had I been on a run in my home area I would have limped home and ended the day with a sense of frustration. However, I had been forced to keep going, had picked up the pace, and covered at least 12km. I bumped into my hotel unexpectedly, and so ended the day in a very cheerful mood.

It's a funny old game, running!

Rugby in Riga

David

I SPENT TWO WEEKS working in Riga last February.
In the depths of winter it is a scary place for a runner.
Although the snow-covered roads, pavements and paths are
strewn with gravel and it is possible to run in the evenings
by reflected light, it is definitely scary. The snow is solid
from the hard frosts and forces you to run with a tentative,
tip-toe motion so that you can cope with a slither or lurch.
It's even scarier running on the treadmills in Hotel Latvia.
The fitness centre is on the 18th floor, and the machines stand
in front of the glass walls, facing outwards. It is as near to
running over a cliff as I ever want to be!

On Saturday I was free; my main desire was not a
daylight run, it was a TV set which would pick up the rugby
international, Scotland v. Wales, from Murrayfield. As kick-
off time approached I was in my room, channel-flicking
furiously. Eurosport had some snowboarding competition
from Slovenia, and the only other sport I could find was a
ladies' soccer match in Italy. I gave up in disgust, put on my
cold weather gear and went for a run.

It was a frosty day with a deep blue sky, and I soon forgot
my frustration. I followed my nose and jogged into Old
Riga, choosing well-preserved cobbled streets with tall
buildings, the former homes of the rich Hanseatic merchants
of earlier years. I passed under the walls of the old castle,

and the old Munitions Tower, which is now the Latvian Military Museum. After 40 minutes or so I turned for home and found myself outside a pub—an Irish pub, to be precise. I stopped and peered in through frosted glass. Yes! I saw a wall-mounted TV with green grass and little red and dark blue figures milling about—they were showing my rugby match!

I went in. The place was quiet, but one table in front of the screen was fully occupied. There were six young Welshmen wearing red and white scarves, each with a large beer in front. I noticed from the screen that it was almost half time, and Wales were winning, but the lads were strangely subdued. I asked if it was a good game, and they nodded, then asked me to join them. I sat down with a glow of happiness.

We turned our attention from the game at half time. The lads explained that it was Thomas' stag weekend, and that they had been in a nightclub called Babylon for most of the previous night, where a good time was had by all. They had slept long and arrived at the pub just a few minutes before I had. They intended to watch this match and both of the other matches scheduled for the next day in this pub. I explained why I was in sports kit, and suddenly a beer was placed in front of me.

"Churlish to refuse," I thought, and that was the end of my run! We watched the second half together and although Scotland made a good fight of it, Wales won convincingly. The tension caused us to slurp rather than sip, and the Latvian barman was quick to replenish. By full-time the lads had regained their spirits and found their singing voices, and it was my round. I went to the bar and told the barman I had no money but would like seven large ones. I showed him my hotel room key, and he poured the beers without a second thought.

Later, much later in the evening, I had a hard job to make my excuses, as the lads were keen to show this poor defeated Scot the delights of Babylon. After fond farewells I waved the barman a promise to return and escaped from the pub. Outside it was dark and bitterly cold. Fine snowflakes drifted lazily in the still air. Breathing in the cold soon brought my brain into sharp focus, and I was able to trot back to my hotel without a problem.

The next day I went back to settle up and re-join my new friends. In daylight, and sober as a judge, it took me over an hour to find the pub, which says much for my homing instinct of the previous evening. It was worth it, as I saw France v. Italy and England v. Ireland; both cracking matches, but I sat alone. This time Thomas and his pals didn't make it to the pub at all.

Sarajevo with Echoes of the Past

David

OUTWARDLY SARAJEVO HAS RECOVERED
well from the war which ended a mere 11 years ago.
There are many new buildings, of course, and the bullet and
shell scars on the old buildings seem like old wounds best
forgotten. Our hotel was right in the centre—Green Beret
Street. The end of this narrow road reminded visitors of
another conflict; a small museum stands here to show that
this is where Archduke Ferdinand was assassinated in 1914.
The street had a supermarket, hotels, coffee shops and
hairdressers and, directly opposite our hotel, a pub from
which came the throb of loud pop music deep into the night.

The December weather was wild, wet and windy, but not
running was not an option! My Swedish colleague Olof and
I had two runs through the city which offered poignant
reminders of the 90s war.

Our first run was to climb the slope which we could see
from our adjacent hotel room windows. Over the Miljacka
River the buildings clung to the lower part of a steep hillside,
then gave way to grassy banks and trees—an obvious
runners' target! Well jacketed, hatted and gloved, we
plodded up the main street, then threaded our way round the
highest houses until we reached a muddy path. We followed
it up to the tree line, where we met a track coming up from
the left. As we still had some wind in our lungs we

73

continued uphill to the right. With no warning at all, we came across the bob and luge runs of the 1984 Winter Olympics. Two concrete U-shaped tracks on pillars wound their way down the hillside, in some places flat, but mostly banked to form a wall. The place was derelict, the structures in ruins; there would be no more bob or luge competitions here for a while. The smooth inner walls were covered in graffiti, and in the concrete were many holes and splatter scars the size of soup plates. The track which led us here had become a concrete road; it also showed obvious bomb and rocket damage. Olof pointed out that the land which dropped off on the other side of our track was roped off with red tape and warning signs of mines. In a sober mood we jogged back down to our hotel. We later learned that these concrete runs had formed the front line between attacking Serbs and defending Muslims for more than three years during the siege, which lasted from April 1992 to February 1996.

The second run was behind our hotel, up the opposite hillside to our first run. Here there was no main street to give us a steady stride, and we had to dodge parked cars, moving cars and other pedestrians. Thankfully the steepness of the streets meant that there were few cyclists to avoid. As we left the cluttered city centre we encountered mosques on most prominent corners, and near to the mosques were cemeteries. No high wall separated these from passers-by and we could read the names and see the photographs of the deceased on the white tombstones. By far the greatest number gave the years of death to be 1992, 1993 and 1994. There is little risk of young Muslims in Sarajevo growing up in ignorance of the city's recent history. Once again we returned to the hotel deep in thought.

Yes, outwardly Sarajevo bustles; the city newspaper *Dnevni Avaz* boasts a modern glassy skyscraper, the streets are filled with new cars, the population young and well-dressed and there are few beggars. For runners, however, the reminders of the recent bloody conflict, in which 12,000 people died, are not hard to find.

Slovenian Rhapsody

Fiona

THE **LJUBLJANA MARATHON** is fantastic! Unlike many others who come to the historic capital of Slovenia, the overriding memories I have of my visit there are not of the castle, cobbled streets, interesting cuisine and beautiful architecture, but of these four things: an Irish coach party, Viking hats, a frenzied horse and the verb to 'trephine'.

It was 2005 and I was meeting my brother and sister-in-law at the City Hotel in Ljubljana on Friday evening before the marathon on the Sunday. They had driven from their home in Bavaria and I had flown from Gatwick on a plane so small and light that it seemed to bounce its way over the Alps, throwing all sixteen of us and our coffee cups around the place like never before. However, all three of us arrived in the Slovenian capital safely and in great form, eagerly anticipating our exciting marathon weekend.

Over breakfast on the Saturday we planned our day and agreed that a quiet day, not too much walking, a good carbohydrate supper, no alcohol and an early night would set us up well for the following day. We decided to register early, to collect our goodies and ensure we were fully prepared and equipped for the race. Having done that, we wandered around the city, took in some of the spectacular sights and enjoyed a long, lazy lunch in the sunshine. Later on, with tickets for the pasta party in our back pockets, we strolled to the open air venue where we found long trestle tables laden with huge containers of plain pasta and a few pots of sauce at the end to add a bit of flavour. We soon noticed that our neighbours on the table beside of us were unlikely to be running the marathon the next day as they were at least half a bottle of vodka for the worse and quite likely 'of no fixed abode'. We looked about to double-check we were in the right place and had not accidentally stumbled across the city soup kitchen as we felt that we 'athletes' were in a great minority when measured against the other, slightly less fragrant diners. We ate our pasta but did not linger for long. We decided instead to try to find a little cafe for a sweet, rich pudding to take on a few final calories. We were soon sitting 'al fresco' under heat lamps in a picturesque café, enjoying a lovely view over the river whilst tucking into chocolate cake and a delicious Slovenian version of raspberry cheesecake. By now it was past 9 p.m. and our early night was beckoning. On entering the hotel we were met by the unexpected yet magnetic sound of live singing coming from the bar area. We couldn't resist popping our heads around the door to investigate further. What we discovered was a bar full of Irish holidaymakers on a coach tour of Slovenia, fully enjoying the fact that Guinness and Irish whisky were served at the bar, and proudly taking it in turns to sing Irish folk songs. We just had to join them! With beer in hand we took a seat and lapped up the atmosphere being created by this happy, tuneful and passionate coachload of singers. By midnight we agreed that we would have just one final drink for the road!

The next morning after a refreshing shower, good breakfast and lot of water to offset the indulgences of the night before, we got chipped-up, greased-up, numbered- and laced-up ready for the big race. For some peculiar and unexplained reason, we decided to wear tartan Viking hats to the start of the race. We have photographs of my brother and me standing outside the hotel, then en route to the start, in the starting 'pens' and even a mile or two into the race still proudly sporting these Viking hats! To this day we don't really remember the significance of them or even where we got them from. The Irish contingent, perhaps?

The marathon route was just as I like it—quiet, rural, interesting; varying from parkland to quiet residential streets and from farmyards to dual carriageway—twice. After one lap of the course the half marathon runners ran jubilantly to their finish while the rest of us (only about 400) pressed on into lap 2. It was on this second lap that the third unusual occurrence in Ljubljana reared his head—literally. It came in the form of a large grey horse that had taken objection to his sleepy little farmyard and peaceful surroundings being overrun by lycra-clad, sweaty, panting runners. Just as I was approaching the farm, I saw this horse leap over the fence from his field into the courtyard through which I was about to run. With a thin field of runners in the race there were only one or two people between me and this beast and they were beginning to stall and falter, wondering how best to get past this unexpected obstacle. At this stage the horse had become very excited and was rearing up and kicking all over the place; with ears pinned back and a menacing look in his eyes, he wasn't an animal any of us really wanted to mess with! Fortunately a farmer appeared and managed to shoo the horse into a corner just in time for me to pass by, but I'll always remember that image, and feel I owe that horse a note of thanks for giving me a bit of a spring in my step just as I needed it most.

On finishing the marathon, I met up with my brother and his wife and we chatted excitedly about our experiences on the way back to the hotel. My brother was hoping for a sub 3 hour time and missed it by a whisker and I (with a start number of 355) had a chip time of 3hrs 55 minutes. This meant there were no PBs for the family that day, but we were happy with how things had gone and delighted it was all over! It wasn't until the adrenalin began to ebb away and the high of holding the medal in my hand began to wear off that the pain in my toes began to set in. On taking off my shoes, I remember vividly my brother gasping as he saw my blood-stained socks and black toes. One crucial part of marathon preparation had been overlooked. I had failed to ensure my toenails were adequately trimmed, causing a build-up of blood under the nail of each big toe.

Painkillers, a few celebratory glasses of wine and the 26.2 miles in my body meant I slept well that night and managed to board the return flight on my little plane to Gatwick very early on the Monday morning. However, the pain then became unbearable and I took myself straight to Accident and Emergency to receive some sort of relief from this pounding pressure in my toes. After just a short wait, a nurse invited me through to the treatment room where he picked up a paperclip from his desk, opened it up to create a long metal rod, wrapped a bit of gauze and plaster around one end as a 'handle' and then proceeded to heat the other end, using his cigarette lighter. When the tip was red hot he simply sank it into the middle of my toenails, taking a sudden step to the side to avoid the fountain of blood going straight into his face. With the surgical procedure over, he gave me a piece of paper to return to the front desk which simply said 'Both big toes successfully trephined'. That was a new word to me and one that I will now always associate with Ljubljana.

So, Irish singers, Viking hats, horse and toes... but I would also vouch for the wonderful city of Lubljana, its picturesque setting, the welcoming people and for hosting one of the most enjoyable, better-organised marathons I have ever experienced.

The Last Laugh

David

FOR THE MONACO MARATHON we rented an apartment in Mougins, just behind Cannes and handy for both Monaco and Nice Airport. My wife and I arrived first, eight days before the race. We had the prospect of a few days exploring the area and ferrying the others from the airport as they arrived. I also planned a few gentle training runs, despite the cold, wet weather.

Our part of Mougins was on a steep hillside. The lanes which led to the top were very steep and too narrow to have pavements, and so unsuitable for safe jogging. Lower down, where the slope became gentler, some equally narrow lanes twisted between the rocky garden walls of grand houses. I found that, by rising early and catching the lanes free of vehicles, I could run here safely. Mougins is a fashionable art colony, and boasts some well-heeled residents who seem to like long lie-ins, so early vehicle traffic was light.

One morning I chose a pleasant lane, with beautiful houses on either side. The walls were high, but there were also gates through which I could gaze admiringly at the buildings within. As I relaxed into a comfortable, rhythmic stride I felt good, and made a mental note to bring the others down this lane the next morning. Suddenly my reverie was shattered. Without any warning a large, brown dog threw itself at a small metal-frame gate at the precise moment

81

when I was passing, less than a yard away. As an ambush, the timing was superb! I watched in shock as the dog rushed the gate repeatedly, snarling and barking furiously, jaws slavering in excitement, paws jabbing through the bars. The gate was locked, I noted thankfully, as I jogged away with mixed emotions. I was relieved not to have been torn apart by this hound, but resentful that my peace and rhythm had been so rudely disturbed.

The next morning there were four of us running this route, and I primed the others: "That house with the pine tree has a guard dog, and it will probably be waiting for us. If it rushes the gate and barks at us, why don't we rush the gate from our side and shout back at it!"

Sure enough, the dog repeated its performance of the previous morning, and we shouted back at it, in poor French and rude Anglo-Saxon. The dog disappeared, and we started off again triumphantly. Ten yards beyond the small gate we came to a large drive-in gate… wide open! Our dog stood square-legged on the imaginary boundary line between his property and the road, and growled at us, a deep menacing growl. As he seemed to know his legal limitation, we slid gently past him, muttering "Good dog, bon ami…" until round the next bend.

The look of contemptuous superiority on that dog's face remained fixed in my mind as we sprinted the next mile!

Side-tracked in Slovakia

David

IN MAY 2008 we were conducting a 2-week course in the
centre of Trenčin, a bustling town in western Slovakia.
We were booked into Hotel Flora in Cingov, some 12
kilometres from Trenčin, and ferried to and from there by
minibus. While some complained at being away from the
bright lights, I, the only runner in the team, was delighted.
Hotel Flora was in the Nizke Tatra National Park, and was
surrounded by rolling wooded hills—ideal running terrain!
As we took breakfast at 8 and boarded the minibus at 8.30 I
would rise at 6 and enjoy an early morning run. There were
paths in all directions, the trees were alive with warbling
birds and the weather was perfect. What a start to the day!

In the second week my routes became more ambitious. I
rose earlier and ran farther. I was told that if I ran up the road
for 6km I would come to a lake, the path round which was
about 4-5km. So, there was a tasty run of 17km! I chose
Thursday, the day the Minister for Education was to visit our
course, and set off at 5.30, giving me plenty of time to cool
down and shower before breakfast. I reached the lake in good
fettle, and was about to swing off to the right along the
lakeside path when I spotted a sign at a narrow road heading
in the opposite direction: "To the American War Memorial." I
hesitated, then curiosity triumphed, and I headed left. The
road led up a peaceful valley with wood and fields and

ribbons of sleepy hamlets. After half an hour or so it occurred to me that I had no idea how far the memorial was from the road, but I could see the valley narrowing ahead, and carried on. I soon reached the end of the road at a turning circle. A path led upwards through the trees and the logical move was to follow it. A niggling thought that I might be pushed to return in time for breakfast was brushed aside. I remember the words of the French mountaineer Lionel Terray when caught on a severe rock climb: "To go on was impossible, to turn back, unthinkable," and I continued uphill. The path became steeper, and I could see that I was approaching a treeless ridge. At the apex of the slope was a small but poignant memorial. It was a wooden post driven into the ground, with a propeller bolted into it horizontally to form a crude cross. At the foot was a circle of twisted aluminium and steel, and a small plaque giving the names of two airmen and the date, 11 April 1945. I looked around at the peaceful scene and tried to imagine the horror of a crashing aircraft, especially tragic so late in the war.

I glanced at my watch and was shocked to read 7.15! I had run 6km north up the road, then west up the track for 30 minutes—say another 5km.... Yes, I had a serious time problem! I noticed an inviting path which led from the ridge in a south-easterly direction, and, confident that I could cut a corner on the way back, set off with some urgency. The path soon plunged downhill into another valley, which curved round to the west, so I chose a narrow animal trail which took my southeast line. This path climbed steeply out of the valley and onto another ridge where it disappeared. I held my south-eastern line and slalomed down through the dense wood into yet another valley with no sign of human presence at all. At 7.40 I was desperate and spending much more energy that was good for me. When I crashed through some bushes and found myself on a rough track I said a short prayer of thanks and bolted along it, thankfully in a southern direction. There was no sign of the road between the hotel and the lake, so I guessed that I was still a valley short. Where I could see a dip in the ridge to the east, I shot off uphill again. As I crested the ridge I could hear the rumble of a truck below, which gave me reassurance that I was heading for home. I reached the road with less than 1km to run, and entered the lobby of the hotel just as my team was emerging from breakfast at 8.25. My legs were scratched, my kit drenched with sweat and my face a deep red. No words were needed; I gave a wave of apology and trotted up to my room. When I came down dressed and slightly less red, it was 8.45. Before I could blurt out my tale, I was told that the minibus had broken down, and would not arrive until 9.30! Furthermore, the Minister had been in contact to say that he would not be able to visit us after all. I went back upstairs and lay on my bed until my heartbeat settled down to its normal rhythm.

Thanks to the non-arrival of the Minister we were able to make up the lost time and the day finished back on schedule. I took an early night, and the next morning shuffled round a short, circular route which never took me more that 1km from the hotel.

I had learned my lesson.

AMERICAS

Gaspin' in the Aspen 15K

Flagstaff, Arizona
19 June 2010

Paul

AS PART OF BUILD UP for the Run with The Devil Marathon, I decided to enter this race as my last (and to be honest, only) bit of speedwork. I've always wanted to run in Flagstaff. Despite being only 100 miles from desert on all sides, the high altitude (8,000 ft) has blessed the town with Alpine-style conditions and beautiful aspen forests with literally hundreds of miles of trails which become cross-country ski trails in the winter.

I was camping at the South Rim of the Grand Canyon, just 60 miles away, so I didn't have the best of sleeps the night before, not least because I was wakened at 2 a.m. by the piercing screams of a pack of coyotes attacking something (I don't want to know what).

The race started at 8 a.m. at the Flagstaff Nordic Centre and was run on undulating terrain, partly trails and partly open forest. There were lots of rocks and logs to hurdle constantly, which made things more interesting, especially on the steep downhill sections.

I'd never run at altitude before and I was in for a bit of a shock when the race started. The first thing I noticed was that everyone had one, sometimes two, big bottles of water. For a 15K!? Yep. The second thing that jumped out at me was the fact that I would be hitting an aid station every 3k! At the time I thought this was being overly protective of the runners, but after the first couple of miles, I was thankful for the multiple opportunities to rehydrate/take a breather!

Its one of the weirdest feelings when running, knowing that you are pretty fit but struggling to find your breath on even the slightest of inclines. The first mile was flat, relatively straightforward, but my breathing was more laboured than normal. As soon as we hit the first hill, climbing 300ft, I was in trouble. I had to walk portions of every single hill as I literally couldn't catch my breath.

The cross-country/downhill portions, though, were a different matter. I cruised down these and they were so much fun, especially the portions where there was no trail and you just had to make your way downhill as best you could!

The last mile was all downhill on a nice flat trail and, despite promising myself to take it easy and not do anything stupid like turn an ankle or something, I opened up and tanked it to the finish line! I finished 8.97 miles in 1:06:43. Almost a 7:30m/m average which I was delighted with, given the fact that it was the hardest race I'd run in a while. I understand now why athletes train at altitude. Getting used to running at 8000ft must make running at sea level a piece of cake! Despite walking some of the hills, I finished 10th overall, so was really chuffed.

Angel's Landing

Zion National Park, Utah, USA

David

"**A**ND ON THE LEFT**,**" drawled our courtesy bus driver, "is Angel's Landing." She indicated a huge pillar of red rock which rose majestically from the canyon floor. "There is a trail to the top, but it is only for experienced hikers, with chains and iron ladders near the top. Part of the route is a series of switchbacks known as Walter's Wiggles, after the trail builder."

Our family group went to the top end of the canyon, and enjoyed some gentle hikes to the Weeping Wall, Hanging Gardens and Emerald Pools before lunch and a return to the hotel. The next day was to be our last, when we had to drive back to Las Vegas and fly back to the UK, so I hatched a cunning plan. Over supper I explained what I wanted to do, and, thanks to the white wine, had my plan approved.

I rose at 5 a.m. and slipped out of the hotel. The first courtesy bus left the Information Centre at 5.15, and I was on it. Half a dozen others climbed in; all had Angel's Landing in their sights, but they were all dressed for a day hike, whereas I was in my running kit. My aim was to tackle this peak at speed, and to be back at the hotel in good time for the return journey.

At the Grotto bus stop I sped off, ahead of the others. The trail started gently, heading for the gap between Angel's Landing and the main massif. Before long I reached some switchbacks, beautifully constructed so that I could continue my jogging pace. I reached the gap in good time, to find that the trail contoured round the base of the vertical cliff of Angel's Landing. I ran swiftly along the trail, still in shade, until it turned sharply to the right. I had reached Walter's Wiggles! If you know the impossibly steep Lombard Street in San Francisco, think of this converted into a concrete-floored hiking trail and made even steeper. I slowed to a fast walk but, thanks to the excellent design of the trail, gained height quickly.

Pleased with my progress, I emerged onto a gentle slope (with restrooms!) and started jogging again on the main trail. It curved round to the left, and was a pleasant, easy climb for a km or so. I reached a summit with a sign, and was perplexed to read: "West Rim Spring." This was unexpected! I turned round. Behind me, and much lower, I could see the obvious peak of Angel's Landing! I dashed down to the top end of the Wiggles, and there was a sign which I had missed: Angel's Landing—down to the right. Now I had a time problem. I went down to the saddle and started picking my way through the rocks to the narrow ridge which led up to the peak. Over steeply slanting slabs I hauled my way along chains, and scrambled up rocky ledges. Then I stopped. This was not a route to hurry along, neither climbing up nor down, and I was in a hurry. I agonised briefly, then started back. Mission aborted. By now I had to pass by others on the ridge, and the delays brought by doing this safely, confirmed that I had made the right decision. Once back on the main trail I loped downhill, passing several panting groups on their way up, and caught a bus back down the canyon. I reached the hotel just in time for a shower before the family breakfast, and we started the long journey home as planned.

I did not reach the summit of Angel's Landing that morning, but I had a great early morning run, and now have a very good reason to go back.

"It started when.....?"

Gheral Brownlow Memorial 10K, Prescott, Arizona
4th July 2009

Paul

ONE OF THE DOWNSIDES of entering a race while on holiday abroad, is having to be good and restrained for a couple of days beforehand to make sure you are in peak physical condition on the day. Unless, of course, you stumble across the grand opening of a new Irish bar the day before! I found myself in this situation the day before the Gheral Brownlow 10k, and my decision to enjoy the free Guinness would come back to haunt me. I was staying in Glendale, Arizona, the night before the race. Being around 100 miles south of the course proved to be a blessing as I had to be relatively well-behaved to be able to drive up on the morning of the race. Still, with hindsight, it wasn't the best of pre-race preparations!

The race started at 7 a.m. on the morning of 4th July, a great way to kick off Independence Day celebrations. I was up at 4.30 a.m. to get to Prescott in time. The sun was already coming up and it was looking set to be another hot, blue-sky day in the desert. The drive up was spectacular, and the breathtaking scenery quickly dissipated my tiredness.

The Gheral Brownlow 10k is a true community event, named in honour of a local man, loved by the whole town, who sadly lost his fight against cancer the year before. In Prescott Gheral Brownlow was a community leader and keen sportsman. He helped to set up community baseball and other sporting schemes and spearheaded the creation of Pioneer Park in the town, where the race was held, which was created completely by volunteers.

The race was held on the aptly named Brownlow trail, a 6-mile sandy, hilly trail around the park, built by Gheral Brownlow himself. I arrived there at 6:45 a.m. just in time for the race to start, or so I thought. This is where my preparations failed me, for the race actually started at 6:30 a.m.! I thought the start area was rather quiet when I arrived!

Luckily the race, although small, had a chip-timing system, so I thought (again wrongly) that my late start would not affect my eventual time. I was even cheeky enough to take an extra five minutes for a few strides of a warm-up. It was only when I stepped up to the start that I realised the chip timing system was only recording final times and not start times!

So, already 20 minutes behind, I set off on my lonely run around the park. My spirits weren't dampened, though. I was already experiencing the friendly, family atmosphere that has stayed with me ever since. In the spirit inspired by Gheral Brownlow, the race is organised and run by local volunteers. The aid stations were set up and staffed by families, with the kids handing out water and the parents providing encouraging words to every runner. In fact, this didn't feel like a race at all. A lot of the participants were walking from the start. This was actually more of a family holiday event, with everyone getting into the 4th July spirit.

Still, I wanted to set a good pace and see if I could catch anyone up and get into the racing pack before the end of the race.

The course itself was very tough. The race is held in the high desert of Arizona, meaning that the temperatures were not as high as those I had experienced at the Run with the Devil 10k the week before. Still, the temperatures were already in the high 20s and there was absolutely no wind. On top of this, the trail was loose, sandy and hilly all the way around, like running on the beach. This quickly zapped energy from my legs and I soon realised why many runners slowed to a walk on the hills.

Within two miles I started passing those at the back of the pack and the sight of runners ahead provided good motivation throughout the race. Almost everyone I passed gave me good encouragement, and I did likewise. Miles 4 and 5 were the hilliest and by far the toughest. The route crossed under the main highway, where the scenery was not so picturesque! With one mile to go, we re-crossed the highway and crested the last of the hills. At this point, the surrounding landscape opened up in front of me and I was treated to the most magnificent view of the Prescott valley. This brought on my second wind and I started rueing the fact that the race was almost over. It was all downhill to the finish and I found an extra bit of energy to finish strong, in front of a surprisingly large, cheering crowd.

My watch time was 40:33, enough on the day for second place overall. Unfortunately, due to the chip timing system, and my late start, my official time was 1:04:09, finishing in 64th position! Turns out that Guinness, for all its good carbohydrates, is not the best pre-race fuel!

Still, the friendly, welcoming feel of this race is one I've never forgotten. It is a perfect example of what 4th July is all about in America. Times and positions didn't matter. Gheral Brownlow would be proud of the manner in which his sporting legacy is being continued by the community.

64th position - 1:04:09. Actual Time - 40:33. Number of Runners – 83.

California Streaming

13 miles from Union Square to Golden Gate Bridge and back
28th January 2008

Frank

THE **TWO EX-COLLEAGUES** now living in San Francisco, who had been enthusiastic earlier in the week to accompany me, had called off when the forecast storm hit. So, at the end of a week in San Jose manning a stand at a trade show, I was on my own again for my annual "half-marathon" from Union Square down Market Street to the Embarcadero, along the Bay and Marina Drive around to Fisherman's Wharf, through the Presidio to the Golden Gate Bridge, and over it to Sausalito and back.

This year was very different from last. In 2007 I'd run it with dawn breaking over the bay, blue skies and still crisp air, the sound and smell of the ocean breakers crashing from the Pacific onto the rocks and the beach and lots of other runners and cyclists out and about before heading to work. This year there was a severe weather warning; huge amounts of rain had already flooded streets and continued to pour down throughout the morning accompanied by gale-force winds. But I had to do it—my Runner's World schedule for preparing for the London Marathon told me so and I had enjoyed it so much the previous year.

The halfway point is an unusual one; I ran to the end of the trail in The Presidio Park and then I was at the foot of the Golden Gate Bridge. I climbed up 250 feet of stairs and then onto the bridge and over it—a horrendous noise from five lanes of traffic that even Californication at full blast on the iPod couldn't begin to drown out! The height of the bridge meant that the full blast of the storm was driving horizontal rain stinging into my face. So it was a case of pulling my hat down over one side and running with a hand up to hold it in place. The bridge is 1.7 miles long and I had the cycle path to myself. No-one else in the entire exercise-obsessed city was out this morning. And then back along basically the same route, almost 2 hours in total—about 20 minutes longer than I'd normally take for that distance due to the conditions.

I had time for breakfast, after which a taxi took me to the airport for the flight home. I mentioned to the driver who was struggling in the wind and rain to keep his car on the road how I'd spent the morning. He was incredulous and thought the TV news should do a story on me. Checking in at KLM, I discovered they wanted me to pay $50 to import rain into Scotland—my bag was overweight as all my running stuff was soaked and I hadn't had time to do anything except seal it in plastic bags. Fighting against time I had to wring out my clothes in the restroom, repack and wear as much clothing as possible and transfer heavy items to every pocket. Although the case was still a pound or so over the limit, the check-in clerk looked at my glowing face and Michelin-man shape and let it go without excess payment.

Exhausted and cocooned, I slept most of the way back to Scotland.

Run with the Devil Marathon

Boulder City, Nevada
26 June 2010

Paul

FOR THE FIRST TIME in a long time, I was seriously nervous about this race. I hadn't felt such nervous excitement since my first marathon. As it was back then, this race was a compete unknown and the likelihood of me even finishing was around 50:50. To put it in context, this marathon was run along a paved road in the Mojave Desert, just outside Las Vegas. It is run in the heat of the day with temps guaranteed to be over 100 degrees and expected to be around 110. In the end, the temp was 108 when I finished just after 2 p.m.

I had been a lot more thorough in my preparation for this race than normal, given the temperatures involved. I had been getting advice from a guy who had run Badwater and he provided me with the invaluable advice of getting regularly to a sauna for the month beforehand so that I could acclimatize as much as possible to the dry heat conditions. This proved to be a vital training aid in the end as, without doing this, I doubt I would have even made it halfway.

In the week leading up to the race, I realized a dream by running a small part of the Badwater course in Death Valley to get my first real experience of running in the heat. Small is the vital word here. I could only manage two-mile out and back portions as, after one mile I had almost run out of water, despite carrying a 600ml bottle. And the heat (estimated around 114F) was stifling, making it hard to breathe. Even wearing an ice-bandana around my neck (my new favourite running accessory!) I was unable to keep cool as the ice had completely melted within minutes. Still, I consoled myself with the knowledge that it probably wouldn't be that hot, come race day.

So, after all of the research, sauna training and acclimatisation, and of course the miles, race-day came around. I was pretty sad to leave Las Vegas the day before. I felt like a bit of a fraud, spending three days in the party capital of the world and not even having one beer! I did get to watch the Soccer World Cup game, US vs. Algeria, with lots of US fans which was pretty amazing. It was probably for the best that the Ghana game was on during the race.

I made my way from Las Vegas to Boulder City, taking the long route along Lake Mead so that I could drive the first and last 10 miles of the course. It was a LOT hillier than I remembered last year when I ran the 10k.

I got up at 6 a.m. with the race starting at 10, and headed to the lake around 9. I wasn't nervous at all. I was really up for it, actually. I knew it would be tough but I'd worked so hard to get my body as ready as possible for this day. It felt like there was so much riding on the day and I was ready to give it my all.

This was the first race where I've had to 'weigh in' at the start. It felt a bit strange weighing in with all these well-tanned ultra and triathletes looking on. God only knows what they were thinking when this skinny pasty-white guy walked up! I weighed in at exactly 140lbs (10st). I was told that I would have to weigh in at the halfway point also, to make sure that I hadn't lost a dangerous amount of weight!

I had 45 minutes to pass so I spent all my time making sure I was covered head to toe in factor 50, constantly drinking and going to the loo, and eavesdropping on the other runners talking about Western States, Badwater, and various other crazy races and triathlons.

The marathon runners were assembled at the start around 9.50 a.m. We were given a race briefing by Joyce, the race director, roughly along the lines of 'please don't die or be run over' and we were off dead on 10 a.m.

Okay, plus points first... the first mile was okay! Except that with all of my drinking and peeing and eavesdropping before the race, I forgot to warm up. As soon as we hit the first hill, my Achilles ached. After a mile I also got pins and needles in both feet. Luckily, we would be hitting an aid station every three miles so I stopped at the first station to re-adjust my trainers and have a quick Achilles stretch. Problem solved.

Three miles in, the temperature was already starting to take its toll. It was around 100 at the start of the race and after only a few miles, I was feeling the heat. Each aid station, however, had ice buckets and everything you could possibly dream of (water, Gatorade, Heed, suncream, pretzels, PB&J sandwiches, Gummibears and loads of gels and powders). The organisation and volunteers were truly amazing, known as the 'angels' of the race. They lived up to their name.

I left the first aid station refreshed and cooled down thanks to dunking my hat and ice tie in ice water—bliss! The Achilles ache and pins and needles had gone and I felt very comfortable. In fact, I was running well within myself for the first half of the race. My whole time was spent making sure I was cool and comfortable. The running part felt like just a side issue.

I soon realised why there were aid stations every three miles. After dunking my hat in ice water, putting ice cubes under my cap and wetting my towel, I managed just under a mile of soothing cool running. After 5-10 minutes, the heat and hot wind had dried absolutely everything and I was back to gritting my teeth and enduring the heat until the next aid station. At the hottest points of the course, there was even an additional bucket placed between aid stations. This was a nice relief, but on the return leg, the water in the buckets had heated up with no shade and was almost unbearably hot!

After 10 miles, we turned off the main lakeside road for the first time and headed over to the mountains. This was mentally the toughest part as you could see the road for miles ahead, winding into the hills.

On the plus side, reaching the turnaround point, I counted six runners passing me in the opposite direction, meaning that I was in 7th place! I weighed in at the turnaround point at 143lbs—a 3lb gain from the start! My hydration strategy was working like a charm.

Up until 13 miles, my legs were still feeling fresh. Upon hitting 15 miles though, they started aching. This is where the real race started. Up until this point I only had to focus on keeping cool, now I had to factor in sore legs. My body was telling me to get to the next aid station a.s.a.p. to cool down and my legs were telling me to slow down. By this point the temperature had gone up a good few degrees and I could definitely feel it. Also, the hot wind picked up quite dramatically so it felt like we were running into a hairdryer on full blast.

I was still in 7th place and I couldn't see anyone behind me so I started walking the hills. The next few miles were really tough. My heart rate was increasing and my breathing was starting to become laboured, even just walking the hills. And it was *so* hot. That probably sounds like I'm stating the obvious but it was even hotter than hot. By the time it got to 1 p.m., I was close to being able to measure the temperatures using the 'gas mark' scale!

At 21 miles, I turned a corner in the road and a beautiful oasis opened up in front of me. We were heading back to the lake. This added to the mental toughness of the race. Lake Mead is a beautiful azure blue lake, very inviting. We were heading downhill and the mirage along the road mirrored the blue of the lake making it look like we were about to run straight into it. If only!

At the 23-mile aid station, I realised for the first time that I was going to make it, even if I had to walk the last few miles. It was only getting hotter and the temperature had gone up a few degrees more. I had kept my decency up until this point but after 23 miles I just didn't care anymore and stripped down to my boxers and dipped everything in ice water. Turns out I wasn't the only one doing this! It made the difference and I was able to keep running the flats and downhills and make an attempt at slow running the uphills.

We summited the final hill at 26 miles and had a nice .2 mile downhill to the finish. I managed a little pick up in pace and crossed the line in 4:16:59 to take 6th place. I headed straight to the ice bath and jumped in. There is no better feeling in the world, honest!

After a few litres of fluid and a hamburger (in typical American style), I was a bit surprised to hear my name being called. Turns out I was the first male under 30 to finish so I got a trophy! This really made my day and, coupled with an ice cold beer, rounded off a perfect race.

Living the Dream

David

MY WIFE PAT AND I were both working flat out that summer. On a rare, quiet weekend we were enjoying an evening in front of the box, watching a travel programme about the Rockies. She beat me by a millisecond to make the comment: A fly-drive holiday in Western Canada would suit us down to the ground! The bookings followed swiftly. As she lived in "nearby" San Francisco, my sister-in-law would be delighted to join us.

It was just a week before the start of our holiday that the reality of the time pressure hit me. I had a huge load of work to complete before I could possibly leave! The pressure concentrated the mind; I sacrificed running, socialising and relaxing, started early, finished late, and on the final day I managed to sign the last letter and leave the last post-it instruction just in time to catch the train home.

The flight was four hours late in leaving Glasgow "because of technical reasons", seats were cramped, the many children restless, and the food, well, disappointing. It was late afternoon before we touched down in Calgary and, with stiff limbs and numb brains, endured a jolly Stampede musical welcome as we emerged with our cases. Sister-in-law Margaret was there to meet us and take us to the car rental. Eventually we were on the road, cruising to our first night's accommodation in the Rockies.

The village of Lake Louise is not at the lake; it is just off the main highway, some 3km in distance from the lake and considerably lower. Our apartment was convenient for the store and Chinese restaurant, where we caught a meal just before it closed. After a short sleep I was wakened by early morning sunlight streaming through a gap in the curtain. I slipped quietly out of bed and dressed in running kit. A quick drink of water, then out into the early morning.

A wide road led uphill to the lake in a series of switchbacks. I chose it rather than the footpath through the woods because of a warning notice telling me that bears had been seen there in the past few days. I'd rather be on a broad road than a narrow path if confronted! After the stress of the last week I realised just how good it felt to be away from work and in such natural beauty. There were conifers on my right, and grassy slopes with bright red flowers (Indian Paintbrush) on my left. As I climbed I saw more and more of the broad valley below, and the rugged peaks on the far side. The feeling of well-being went right through my body, and there was a spring in my step as I levelled out at the grandiose Fairmont Chateau Hotel which fronts the lake.

I stopped at a wooden deck area at 6.30 a.m. and gazed at Lake Louise. It was a cloudless, wind-free day, and the surface of the blue-green water of the lake mirrored the surrounding mountains. To the right was the Beehive, a rugged cone of rock and shrubs, criss-crossed with paths, viewpoints and pavilions; straight ahead stood a forbidding wall of reddish rock broken by white cascades of water, and behind it were the majestic slopes of Pope's Peak and the snows of the Plain of the Six Glaciers. Awesome! as they say in Canada. A path at water level led round the base of the Beehive, and I took it all the way to its end at the far side of the lake. I shared it with one or two other runners and several early-rising photographers. All had the same "Isn't this wonderful?" look on their faces.

The view on the return leg was just as spectacular, with a long jagged line of snow-capped peaks across the valley. When I reached the Fairmont Hotel I was surprised but delighted to see Pat and Margaret near the lake. They, too, had risen early and had driven up for the view. It was good to stop and share it with them, and to record our first morning with the camera. The girls drove and I ran down the hill; we breakfasted, then left to continue our Rockies adventure. We drove north to Jasper, then west to Vancouver and saw some magnificent sights; glaciers, waterfalls, lakes and rivers, bear and moose as well, but that run on the first morning at Lake Louise will remain forever in my mind as the dream start to a holiday.

Nostalgia, Autumn Colours and a Grand Prix Circuit

18 miles through Montreal
9th October 2008

Frank

MONTREAL IS A HEAVILY-WOODED CITY of skyscrapers built on a hilly island surrounded by one of the world's largest rivers, the St. Lawrence. The river is the reason the city exists; it was, until the Lachine Canal was built to form the St. Lawrence Seaway, the furthest point that ocean-going ships could reach. Now the ships can proceed past the Montreal rapids into the Great Lakes. Mont Royal is a 200m high hill in the centre of a park that dominates the city, the highest point of the island. I'd arranged to meet my friend Andy, who lives in Montreal, at the top of the steps leading up to the chalet there at 6.30 a.m. I'd arrived from Schiphol the night before and gone straight out to dinner with Andy from the airport and then to my hotel where I'd slept for a few hours before the 5 hours jet-lag woke me.

After running around the Mont Royal Park a few times, Andy had had enough and went off for breakfast, leaving me to explore alone. I was feeling great! I had lived in Montreal for two years, thirteen years earlier, but hadn't run in those days. Now I had the opportunity to explore some old haunts. A favourite area was a smaller island connected by bridges to Montreal Island—the Ile Notre Dame on which the Formula 1 Grand Prix track and casino are located. I headed there, which meant a run downhill from the park, through the city and across the bridges.

The St. Lawrence is a dramatic river. It drains the North Eastern part of a continent and huge quantities of water flow past Montreal. The view from the bridge is spectacular as the colours of the trees here in the fall rival anything anywhere in the world. I proceeded to the motor racetrack and then ran around it—2.75 miles. This was fascinating for me as I'm an F1 fan. I'd watched three Canadian Grand Prix here from the stands and all the others on TV. I'd been round the track before once on roller blades. No-one else was running—everyone else using the track that morning was a cyclist or roller blader. After one circuit, I was getting hungry, and aware that I had drifted into a longer run than planned. Normally I would have had some food before starting, and some gels in my pockets for a long run, but not today. More glorious tree colours beckoned ahead, but, with a sigh I started the long run back to the hotel, showered and then enjoyed a full Canadian breakfast.

It was good to be back!

To Punta Arenas against the Clock

David

THE FAMILY GROUP had flown from Santiago to Punta Arenas in Chile, down the spine of the snow-capped Andes in bright sunshine—surely one of the most spectacular, beautiful flights in the world. We were still buzzing from the experience as we were whisked by taxi from the small, modern airport into the town.

Three weeks later at the end of our visit we were all leaving on the same day but at different times. First to leave was my sister-in-law, Margaret, bound for the USA. Her flight was to depart at 9 a.m., so she booked a taxi for 7.15 for the journey to the airport. My wife Pat and I were due to leave the hotel at 11 for our 12.45 flight. My offer to accompany Margaret to the airport was a mixture of gallantry and self-interest. I would be useful in carrying her luggage and escorting her to the security gate, but I would also have the chance to stretch my legs, as I planned to run back into town afterwards.

As we set off in the taxi towards the airport we chatted about our holiday, but as the drive continued I felt a certain unease. Exactly how far away was the airport? I only remembered from our arrival that it wasn't "all that far." The taxi driver shrugged and offered: "Veinte...veinte-quatro..." 20..24? It looked as though I—a moderate runner at the best of times—had volunteered for a half-marathon distance! I shared my dismay with Margaret, who offered to give me the return taxi fare, but we runners have our pride. I did accept a small bottle of water from her, however, and left her with more haste than I had planned. I did some calculations. My normal time for a Half was either side of two hours, so... time now is 8.20, so... I should just about be back in the hotel in time to shower and dress. Yes, game on! Off I ran.

It was a beautiful, warm, breezy January morning. From the airport a new road led down to the main coastal highway and, despite the time pressure, I could enjoy the environment. For 10 days we had travelled in a rented van round Patagonia and Tierra del Fuego, and it was wonderful to be running again. When I reached the highway I turned right and felt immediately better. The warm wind which previously had been pushing me to the right was now squarely on my back, urging me forward. The view was dramatic and ever-changing, as I ran past coves and headlands of the broad Beagle Channel. Seals basked or slept on rocks, pelicans and cormorants dried their wings and frigate birds soared overhead. The wind had created a heavy swell on the water which lifted the shiny brown strips of seaweed as it crashed onto the rocky shore. Traffic was light, and the broad pavement deserted, so I could relax and enjoy the scene, sucking in the salty air.

I reached the ramshackle outskirts of the town at 9.50, but it is a long, straggling town, and I still had a long way to go. Fortunately I seemed to have a steady supply of adrenalin. Running with time pressure had me striding purposefully and rhythmically onwards, and I felt that I was floating over the ground. I stayed in this euphoric state until close to our hotel, and then the effort caught up with me and I slowed down to a shambling jog. I reached the hotel at 10.25, went to our room, stripped and dived into the shower. From the streaming water I mumbled an apology to Pat for being later than I had said, while she gingerly packed my sweaty running kit into plastic bags. I had time to eat a late breakfast before we boarded our taxi on the dot of 11. This time I noted carefully the kilometre reading. As I climbed stiffly out of the taxi at the airport I saw that we had travelled exactly 23.6km. I had therefore covered more than a half-marathon in 1 hour 52 minutes.

Pity that it was mainly wind-assisted!

Running Out of Steam

David

IT WAS A SCHOOL EXCHANGE, and we had taken 14 boys to trek in the Canadian Rockies. After an excellent expedition we returned to Calgary, where teachers of the host school entertained us to a barbecue.

After several beers I found myself talking to a very attractive blonde, Becky, who was the Physical Education teacher. When she said how much she enjoyed running I eagerly informed her that running was also an interest of mine. Her eyes opened wide with surprise—I am not built like your typical runner and was several decades her senior. Then she invited me to join her on her early morning run the next day; she would pick me up at six.

As the effect of the beers wore off I reflected on what I had taken on. For the last fortnight I had been plodding under the weight of a heavy rucksack, and, although I had lost a few pounds, I had not run or even jogged for over a month. I retired to bed in thoughtful mood.

At six o'clock I peered out of the motel foyer. A gleaming sports utility with go-faster stripes all over it stood proudly outside, with Becky behind the wheel. There was no backing out.

We drove to the outskirts of Calgary to a wooded hillside ("My favourite route!") and parked in the deserted car-park. Becky started her warm-up, so I did a few stretches and bends, then turned to her expectantly. She seemed to be in a trance and continued a 15-minute sequence of athletic exercises which seriously frightened me. Then she flashed a brilliant smile at me and set off, blonde ponytail bobbing behind her. My fears were soon realised. Becky was much faster, and stronger. I would have to cheat.

Accelerating way out of my comfort zone I drew level with her and asked some crafty questions, which I knew would demand a lengthy answer and interrupt her breathing: "How had she taken up running?" "What was the Stampede like?" "What was the Calgary political situation?"

She answered each one fully and, to my growing dismay, did not start to puff and pant in the slightest. I then tried the old loose shoelace trick, which gained me a few precious seconds of standing in one place. Becky jogged on the spot impatiently.

On we went, and I knew that the pace was at my upper limit for a couple of kilometres at most, and she was talking of running much further. I pointed to a slightly unusual tree, and asked her what it was. For a moment I thought that she would have to stop to examine it before replying, but no! A quick glance and she identified it and named it without breaking her stride. A few minutes later I tried the same question about a small flowering plant by the side of the trail. She paused, frowned and said, "Don't know." We ran on—beauty and the beast.

The trail started to go uphill, but Becky's bobbing stride kept the same rhythm as before. I was getting desperate! Some 15 meters behind her, I wheezed, "Becky! Stop! I think I can hear a cuckoo!"

Becky stopped and looked at me for a long moment. I was not a pretty sight. Perspiration streamed down my face and arms, my chest heaved and my knees were all a-tremble.

"We don't have cuckoos in Alberta, Dave," she said calmly, "and besides, you would never hear them anywhere in the northern hemisphere in September."

However, after that she slowed down considerably, and soon turned for home.

Run of Luck

David

JACK AND I HAD TWO DAYS FREE at the end of our visit to Ecuador. We had "done" most of the major attractions of this delightful country; we had shopped at Otavala Market, climbed an Andean peak where condors soared, camped on the high grasslands, and, down in the Oriente, had stayed in an eco-lodge in the rainforest, panned for gold and rafted on a rushing headwater of the Amazon. On our tight budget, however, the famous Galapagos Islands were a non-starter. We had to go by bus to catch our return flight from the southern city of Guayaquil, but were told that the city had little to offer a tourist.

Where to go?

We had reached the stage on a budget holiday when money is tight and you start counting backwards, starting with airport tax, transport to airport, beds for two nights. Meals would be spartan! We reckoned that we had just enough to go to the seaside town of Manta for the last two days. *The Rough Guide* saw it as "a lively and popular holiday destination" and that was that; we went to Manta.

Our bus dropped us near the harbour at 6 p.m. As we walked to Hotel Pacifico—chosen as the cheapest in the guide book—the mood of keen expectation took a battering. When we crossed the bridge over Rio Manta a glance down to the filthy water was enough to keep us from wanting to swim anywhere near its mouth, while the smell from the fish factories took away any hopes of fresh Pacific Ocean air in our lungs. We dumped rucksacks in our rooms, then Jack suggested we go for a run. We had no running shoes, so headed for the long beach south of the harbour wearing flip-flops. When we reached the beach we would simply wear a flip-flop on each hand like a glove and jog barefoot. As we passed the harbour Jack spotted a yacht *Karin D* with the German flag, registered in Kiel, and commented that this chap was a long way from home.

The run on the long, sandy beach was very good. A gentle sea breeze kept the smell of oily fish away, and there were few people about. The high-water mark was a line of bleached wood, seaweed and plastic, lots of plastic. We found a layer of hard sand just below this line and settled into a pleasant jog. Suddenly my eye was drawn to something in the high-water line. It was a wet green and black day-sack. I have one exactly the same—perhaps that is why I spotted it. I stopped, picked it up and automatically checked it over. I knew that there was a discreet zipped pocket on the outside which is easy to overlook, and I pulled out of this pocket a sodden German passport in the name of Helmut Dittmann. We continued our run, but on the way back stopped at the German yacht. A bearded man wearing only faded blue shorts sat in the cockpit smoking a pipe. He saw us approach and jerked into life when he saw what I was carrying. To cut a long story short, he was overjoyed to be reunited with his passport, and would we come on board for a beer?

Helmut had taught Maths for years in a secondary school in North Germany. His wife died suddenly and he felt the need for a complete change. After selling everything he had, he bought *Karin D* and was sailing her slowly round the world. He would charter when it suited him, otherwise he kept his own company. Two evenings ago he had been walking back to the harbour from a restaurant when he had been mugged. The thief had knocked him to the ground and snatched the day-sack. In it were a camera, some groceries, a German novel and, of course, the passport. Helmut was relieved not to have to go to the German Consulate in Guayaquil to renew his passport, a process which would last weeks rather than days. He asked about us, and we explained that we had opted to chill out on Manta's beaches for our last two days, but were less than impressed with the place. Helmut told us that he and the yacht were at our disposal for the next two days! Furthermore, there was a small island group within a day's sail called Islas de la Plata, which is also called the Poor Man's Galapagos. We should take overnight bags and swimming gear.

We went on board at 10 the next morning and set off under a bright blue sky with the motor purring gently. Soon we stopped the motor and hoisted sail. Helmut proved to be a delightful chap, keen to show his gratitude for the returned passport, and glad of some European company. As we sailed over a rolling sea he pointed out frigate birds, blue legged boobies, dolphins and even an albatross and humpback whales. When we reached the island we moored in a quiet cove and snorkelled with turtles and a colourful collection of tropical fish. We caught snapper and grouper for supper, drank beer and put the world to rights as we watched the sun go down. We sailed round the island on the next day, and returned in good time for our evening bus to Guayaquil.

A simple beach run had led to the perfect ending to our visit to Ecuador. It pays to keep your eyes open when you are out jogging!

10 Kilometers, 32 Degrees, 2nd Place

Paul

TEN MINUTES FROM HOOVER DAM in Nevada on the edge of Lake Mead sits Boulder City. With a population of 15,000 the name is slightly misleading. It is more small town than city, established to provide a settlement for the workers constructing the dam in 1932. Despite its size, it boasts two huge casino resorts and every fast food chain that springs to mind. It really is just a stop-off town for those heading to or from the neon-shimmering spectacle of Las Vegas, only 20 miles away.

Boulder City, however, is the home of a bi-annual series of endurance races: The "Running from an Angel" series in the pleasant winter desert temperatures of January, and the "Running with the Devil" series in the hellish furnace of the Southern Nevada midsummer. On 27 June 2009, I found myself in my running kit at 6 a.m. on the shore of Lake Mead, ready to try my first ever desert race, not-so-fresh from an evening of embracing the indulgences of sin city. The series of races, all run on the same day, consists of a 5k, 10k, half-marathon, marathon and 50-mile race. I opted for the 'easy' option of an early morning 10k which, despite starting at 7 a.m., was still around the 30 degree Celsius mark by the time the gun went off, and at least a couple of degrees hotter by the time I collapsed over the line 39 minutes later.

All races follow the main tourist road around Lake Mead in an out-and-back format. The shimmering, crystal blue waters of the lake create a mental anguish to match the physical pain by taunting every runner from the corner of their eyes as they struggle with an intensely hot, dry climate just a couple of hundred metres from the shore. The complete lack of moisture and the hot wind make breathing difficult. Luckily the outstanding organisation on the day provided excellent water/ice stops every mile or so.

After cheering off the fearless ultra runners, and listening to a rather worrying safety briefing about the dangers of running in the current temperatures, I lined up at the front of 80 or so other runners ready to face the unknown. I foolishly started the race around my normal 10k pace. The heat put paid to that idea within half a mile and I settled into a group comprising the second to fifth placed runners, with the eventual winner gliding away effortlessly into the distance. In the desert climate, it is even more important than normal to make sure that sufficient fluids are taken on board. Despite the relatively short distance of the 10k, I was relieved to find that all the runners around me were slowing considerably, even stopping, at all water stops from the second mile onwards. For me, it took around half a minute at each stop to take on board what I felt was enough water. Within a couple of minutes of every stop, however, the dry wind had sucked all moisture from my mouth and the breathing troubles started again.

Just before the turnaround point, we caught up with the ultra runners who had started even earlier than the 10k runners. I felt like a fraud running past them, knowing that I was going to be finished in another 20 minutes or so and that they had many hours ahead of them. Nevertheless, everyone was in good spirits and we exchanged our 'good luck's. I've always admired ultra runners, but having experienced just 15 minutes of desert temperatures, I was completely in awe of these hardened souls who were all chatting away happily, enjoying every second of the run.

With just under two miles to go, I experienced my first wave of complete exhaustion, but I was in second place and had a 10-15 second lead over the third placed runner. Despite feeling very hot and a little faint, my competitive instincts kicked in and I pushed through a level of discomfort that I'd never experienced before. It wasn't a physical tiredness as such, it was just the heat taking its toll. At several points I seriously contemplated running off course and straight into the beautifully cool crystal blue lake just to my left.

Luckily, the last half mile was downhill and I held it together to maintain second place and collapse over the finish line. The winner had finished in 34:06, some 5 minutes ahead, and he still looked as fresh as a daisy! By contrast, I think my bright red face provided great amusement to the many supporters at the finish. My reward for the previous 39 minutes of hell was a beautiful handmade, Nevada State-shaped slate trophy, which I will be eternally proud to display.

After the most amazing dip in the lake, I took a drive along the 50-mile route to give some support to the real hardcore runners I had just met, before heading back to Las Vegas to celebrate in style!

AFRICA

Cape Town Jan 06

David

WHAT DO YOU SAY TO PEOPLE in the hotel lift when you enter after a long run?

From our hotel window, I could see the 300m-high long back of the "lion", from the eastern end of which protrudes the Lion's Head, a rocky stump which is a prominent landmark to the east of Cape Town. The lion was black, as a recent bush fire had burned every bush and blade of grass on both its flanks, but it beckoned to me, so I had to go there for a run.

I padded over the shining tiles of the lobby to start my run. There was a seminar of British estate agents swarming around the Reception desk; men with short-sleeved shirts and ties, women with twin sets and pearls, all with briefcases and name badges. The road outside was bathed in warm sunlight; I turned right and crossed the busy main street. It became steep almost at once, and before long I had reached its end, where I clambered over a low wall and took a faint track though a belt of pines.

One hour later I returned after a wonderful run which had given me clear views over the sprawling city and port, out to sea and over to Robben Island. Behind was the majestic sweep of Table Mountain without its usual "tablecloth" of cloud. A marvellous run indeed—but at some cost! The dry wind had lifted flakes of burnt wood, ash and soot from the ground I had been running on, and they had stuck onto my perspiring skin. I had brushed against the charred ends of the bush twigs on either side of the path. Some had left red scratch marks, others black streaks. My hair was straggly, my face red from exertion and my shorts grimy and soaked with sweat. My trainers were filthy, of course, and my T-shirt a disgrace.

As luck would have it, the lift, which stopped at the lobby floor for me, already contained some of the estate agents, coming up from the parking level. They quickly hugged the walls of the lift as I entered.

So what do you say?

When we reached my floor I said in a slow voice: "Are you aware that, in South Africa, today is 'Hug a Stranger" Day'?"

There was momentary panic in their eyes before they laughed.

Caught Out in Clarens

David

CLARENS IS A TOURIST TOWN in the Free State, South Africa. It is 1800m above sea level, on the western slopes of the Drakensberg, some three hours' drive from Johannesburg. Tourists love the clean air, the outdoor activities and the thriving artists' colony. It is also one of the best trout fishing centres in Africa.

The drive there had been long and hot, and my wife and I were glad to check into our B&B under cloud cover. After unpacking we set off to explore. There was no risk of losing ourselves as our temporary home lay on Main Street, the spine of the village, rising from Main Square and going straight up to the hills behind. It started to drizzle before we had gone far, so we quickly booked a table for supper in the lively bistro and scurried back to our room. My wife took out her Sudoku book and settled down, but I put on my running kit. Warm rain is better than Edinburgh rain, I thought, so I'll just ignore it.

I ran up the length of Main Street until it ended at a T-junction, unmade roads going left and right. A gate straight ahead gave access to a tempting track into open country. Cloud was low but I could see a horseshoe of hills in front. Lush grazing land gave way to scrub, above which lay steep grassy hillside with sloping slabs of red rock. A path led away from the track to the left ridge of the horseshoe, and I took it. It climbed gently at first, but soon reached the first wide slabs. Someone had used lime-green paint to mark the route over the slabs. It was scuffed and faint, but I jogged confidently along it. Even in the wet conditions the slabs offered good grip. After a while the route steepened, but the paint was still clearly there! Glancing over to my left I was puzzled to see another paint mark. To my right, yet another! I stopped, bent down and peered at the paint. At this range my eyes changed their message to my brain: this is lime-green lichen, and it's everywhere! No harm done, I chuckled, and took the natural line of weakness up the ridge. As I climbed I met strong wind and heavier rain. I had already reached the stage of being so wet that I could get no wetter, so that was no worry. I had spotted a small river, however, between the foot of the right-hand ridge and Main Street, and wondered if the downpour might make my crossing awkward on my return route.

I must have been at the apex of the horseshoe when the thunderstorm reached me. It came over the high mountains to the south and descended angrily onto my hill. The rain hit the ground with such force that it produced a loud hissing sound, punctuated by crashing thunder and vivid sheet lightning. I splashed onwards, keen to descend as quickly as possible. The direct route back to the village was impossibly steep, so I stepped down at an angle which would take me to lower and safer ground. Low bushes tore at my socks and shins, and their thorns prevented me from using them as hand-holds. Long before I reached the river level I heard the roar of its gushing, brown water. To cross here or try further down? The first rule of river-crossing is to find a bridge, so I ran on, 100m or so above the river. A barbed wire fence appeared on front of me, and I hopped over it and continued.

Aha! There was a gate, and a track, so I followed the track until it crossed the swollen river on a solid bridge, and it eventually brought me to the gate at the head of Main Street. The thunderstorm had passed, but the rain poured down relentlessly. The street was deserted as I squelched in triumph and relief back down to our B&B. When I walked into my room—90 minutes after I had left it—my wife raised a sleepy head:

"Good run?"

"Not bad," I replied, "a bit wet."

There are some runs which are amazingly enjoyable, but difficult to explain to non-runners.

Making Friends in South Africa

David

IT **WAS STILL DARK** when I crept out of our B&B in Knysna, South Africa, to go for an early-morning run. It is normal for me to head for high ground in a place I am visiting for the first time, so that is what I did. I found the main road leading inland from the coastal town and was pleased to see that it had a wide pavement on one side, although it was quite steep and winding. A few trucks crawled up the hill, belching diesel fumes, and some laden with fruit and vegetables made for the Knysna market behind me. As dawn broke I found the gradient easing off, and I could make out paths leading away from the road through dense woods. The traffic was becoming heavier, so, on impulse, I took one of these paths. It was a well-trodden line of dried mud which was good to run along. Sadly the sides of the path were strewn with litter. I had run for only 500 meters or so when the trees gave way to an open area—a basketball court, and I realised that I had stumbled into one of the townships for native Africans which surround every sizeable South African town.

The houses were of uniform structure; low plaster walls topped with a corrugated iron roof. There seemed to be activity in and around each house as occupants prepared noisily for school or work. Some waved at me, others looked curiously at me, but I had no feeling of any aggression towards me—a European intruder in their world. A concrete road wound round the hillside so I took it as far as the main exit. I turned down the road towards Knysna and opened my stride to enjoy the downhill run into town.

After a short time I heard the footfall of another runner behind me. I turned and saw, hard on my heels, a gangly African youth in a dark blue suit, white shirt and light blue tie. On his feet were grey socks and black shoes, and under one arm he clutched a battered black briefcase. I waved him through, but he declined, so we ran together.

Joshua worked in a bank and lived in the township I had just left. He loved running, so when he saw me he decided that he would run all the way into town with me, at least 5km! He had left school with good exam results four months ago, and had been at the bank for six weeks. He found the work easy but confided that his manager was a bossy woman who gave him a hard life! He had never been farther away than nearby Port Elizabeth, where he and his schoolmates had taken part in a basketball tournament. I kept looking at his feet: his badly-worn and dusty shoes appeared to be at least two sizes too large for him, his laces loosely tied, and he ran with a high stepping motion. Despite the briefcase under one arm he managed good upper body movement and chatted while breathing easily at what I considered to be a decent pace. When I told him that I live in Scotland his face broke into a wide grin: "Braveheart! My favourite film!" He turned to the roadside trees and shouted at the top of his voice: "Freedom!" then grinned again.

All too soon I reached my turn-off and we stopped and shook hands. He was still grinning, but I was pleased to see that he was also panting a little and his face shone with sweat as he gently strolled the rest of the way down to his bank.

Nearly Lost in Wilderness!

David

WHEN I SAY "LOST" I don't mean "unaware of my exact position", I mean it in the poetic sense, as in "lost at sea". When I say Wilderness, I don't mean an unpopulated and hostile region, I mean the thriving seaside resort of that name, east of George, in South Africa.

My wife Pat and I were on a fly-drive holiday, and had planned a long drive that day, so I rose early for a decent run. The main attraction of Wilderness is a beautiful beach with the Indian Ocean sending in huge, white-crested waves, but I chose an inland route for this run. A brochure had informed me that Wilderness National Park was within reach; just a kilometre or so up the N2 road, turn left at Dumbleton and I would soon be there.

Our B&B was a modern villa perched above the beach. I crept out before 6 a.m. and jogged purposefully up the hill to Dumbleton, then down to the park. I was dismayed to find myself heading for a chain-link fence with a locked gate and a notice saying that payment was necessary, but a side gate was open, and in I went. The sketch map in the brochure had shown a red dotted line labelled the Pied Kingfisher Trail which headed east, turned north, then west and back to the road. I should have noted that the sketch map had no scale on it. Off I went, pleased to have sneaked in without a ticket. Pied kingfishers must be fond of reeds, as the trail was a grassy clearing 2m wide between beds of high reeds. Not much of a view, but some disturbingly heavy rustling noises as some unseen creatures moved off at my approach. For one hour the trail offered me green grass, yellow reeds and a deep blue sky, these colours only, and not a sight of a kingfisher! When I eventually reached each turn of the trail I was relieved, and doubly so when I set foot on the main park road again. I had taken much longer on this trail than I intended, and I was tiring.

When I approached the N2 road it was buzzing with morning commuter traffic. Why not pop down to the beach and run along it, I thought. There was an access path leading down through 50 metres of dunes thickly covered with gnarled bushes, and soon I was jogging along the beach. The sand was soft and sloping, which wakened the memory of a beach run several years ago which had given me an Achilles injury. With a kilometre to go I could either slow down to a walk or nip back up to the road rather than risk injury. The pact made the previous evening with Pat to be at the breakfast table by 8 made me opt for the road.

I climbed a dune of soft sand, and saw the crash barrier of the road 50 metres ahead and slightly higher up. I also saw a dense, green carpet of bushes between me and the road. I moved to the right, and then to the left, searching for a path through the bushes and finding none. Next I looked for a place where the bushes were tall enough for me to creep under, again without success. The bushes were well-established, and thick branches twisted and turned to fill the space between the sandy floor and their flat tops. For some reason the idea of retracing my steps to the access path never entered my head. I could hear traffic on the road above, and thought that surely I could cross over such a short stretch of low bushes! I clambered onto a branch and edged my way forward. After a few steps I noticed that although the top layer of foliage was flat, the ground under the bushes shelved down to form quite a deep valley! Soon I was edging my way over trees which were several metres high.

I was more than halfway across when a branch snapped, pitching me down to my left. My left leg shot downwards on the left side of a strong branch, and my descent was halted by my right leg trying to go down the right-hand side of another branch. My legs were splayed wide with the two branches firmly wedged between. My body had flopped backwards and crashed through some twigs until it came to rest just below the horizontal. In mild shock I lay still for some time, my brain asking all body parts to send in a damage report. Apart from some long scratches on both inner thighs the reports were good; the only problem was that I could not move. I waited until my breathing had settled, listening to the vehicles above, their drivers unaware of this drama just below them. I looked around and chose the branch above me which looked strongest and started to drag myself upwards. Then a resident insect showed its displeasure by biting me painfully on the calf—I had the mark for months afterwards! With my upper body once more above my legs I felt more comfortable, but still firmly wedged. I had now started to contemplate the worst case scenario. Pat knew that I was going to the park, but who would think of looking for me here? If I fell into the dense valley of sand beneath me, could I escape? I pictured the headlines: Scottish Pensioner Injured in Fall from Bushes... or (worse) Elderly Jogger Loses the Plot...

More practical thoughts took over. Hand over hand on branches I pulled my body carefully forward. When it was almost horizontal I could drag one leg loose, then the other. With the utmost care I crawled over the last few metres of treetop and collapsed onto the sandy bank beyond.

The rest of my run was an anticlimax as I limped down the roadside to our B&B. After a civilised breakfast with the other guests (the talk was on cricket, airlines and golf) we said farewell and drove off. I had several angry scratches on my legs and a clicking hip for the next week or so, and that evening I felt very stiff after the long day at the wheel. It may surprise readers to learn that I look on this run as one of the highlights of our holiday, and I intend to return to Wilderness one day to re-visit the scene, but not to attempt the aerial crossing!

MIDDLE EAST &
CENTRAL ASIA

Baku—in Winter and in Summer

David

THE CENTRE OF BAKU is elegant, if somewhat decayed. NATO had chosen for me the optimistically-named Elite Hotel in the suburbs, which had all the decay without the elegance.

My running options from the hotel in winter were before and after the working day, in darkness in both cases. From the airport taxi I had spotted some broad avenues with street lighting near the Hippodrome and not too far away from the hotel, and on my first evening set out to find them. Running on the side of the road is clearly not a popular activity in Azerbaijan's capital city, and no wonder! Pavements were few and far between, and had unguarded holes, angled slabs and broken setts. Exhaust fumes competed with dust from the many road sweepers to clog my lungs, and I had trouble relying on headlights to avoid tripping over the angled wires which supported telephone poles. Retracing the route of my taxi I found the well-lit avenue, which had trees and pathways between the carriageways. For 5 minutes I enjoyed some relaxing running, and even spotted some track-suited joggers, to whom I waved cheerfully. Alas! The well-lit avenue was short, and darkness loomed ahead.

Now I don't know about anyone else, but in a situation like this I am reluctant to retrace my steps. I decided to take a left and after a few blocks, take another left, and I would be back on my outward route, wouldn't I? Dropping back down to my tentative, darkness trot I turned left and felt my way forward. Fortunately a full moon appeared in a cloudless sky. This was not a busy street, and vehicles became fewer. There was a reasonable pavement and I made good progress. After three blocks I turned left and very shortly came to a gate in a high wall. Locked. The wall stretched into the gloom to the left and to the right. Once again my reluctance to turn back pressed me onwards. I spotted a weak point in the wall which had been used by people for access, so in I went. It was the abandoned Russian cemetery. By the moonlight I could see that the graves bore cyrillic inscriptions, but were all horribly vandalised, and I stepped on broken urns, vases and crumbled headstones. My plan was to keep going in the same direction as the street and exit the cemetery at its opposite wall. Eventually I came to another high wall, found a weak point and crawled over. With relief I saw that I was close to my hotel and finished my run at a gentle pace.

I returned to Baku in the summer. NATO had kept faith in Hotel Elite, no doubt swayed by my colleagues who had reported back enthusiastically on the free belly-dancing show! No problems with darkness now, and on my first morning I rose before 6 and set out on my winter route. This morning I had a Swedish chap, Peter, in tow, having promised him an interesting run. I found my way to the cemetery and, as before, we scrambled over the wall. The scene in daylight was one of devastation. What could be smashed was smashed, the rest was daubed with paint—swastikas, slogans and crude drawings. The gravel walkways were weedy and strewn with debris and litter. Rather than take the direct route out we turned down an alley, curious to see more of this unpleasantness. We heard a dog bark. It was a bark of surprise and indignation, and it drew answering angry barks from other parts of the cemetery. At this point my Swedish friend blurted out that he and dogs did not get on well, and could we please find a way out quickly. We "about-turned" and headed for the spot where an exit scramble over the wall was possible. The dogs were gathering and following us, their barks ratcheting up their fury at our intrusion. Peter, who had lagged behind me for most of our run, now showed commendable speed. He crossed the wall commando-style and collapsed, chest heaving on the dusty ground. I was not far behind him, but paused on the top of the wall. There were seven or eight evil-looking street dogs glaring up at me, and, as they could not reach me, seeing me off with a cacophony of snarls and barks.

At breakfast that morning Peter publically thanked me for the "interesting run" but stated that he would not be joining me the next morning, or ever again. In fact, he should have joined me at the weekend, when I met up with the Baku Hash House Harriers. Now there's a wonderful group of people who know how to organise an interesting run!

Running on a Tour of Turkey

David

FOR A REGULAR RUNNER a coach tour presents opportunities and problems. The opportunities are to run in new and exotic locations; the problems are the long daily programmes and the sumptuous buffet meals which deaden the urge to run. Our tour round Turkey in April 2009 lasted 14 days and, with a packed programme of sightseeing, we stayed in eight hotels and covered 2200 miles.

We started in Istanbul, and I managed a run on the first morning. Our hotel was on a ridge overlooking the Golden Horn, so I planned a simple route—down to the waterfront, along the road towards the Bosphorus, then back up to the ridge and our hotel in good time to shower and take breakfast before our programme started at 9 a.m. The streets near the hotel were narrow and winding, but I noted that a nearby white mosque—The Tomb of Suleiman the Magnificent—had scaffolding round all four minarets, an easy landmark to spot if I became disorientated. The route was a good one; under the ancient arches of a Roman aqueduct, down a main road with curious passers-by (running is not very popular in Turkey, I discovered) then along the sparkling water of the Golden Horn, with ferries and pleasure craft preparing for the day ahead. I ran at water level for 15 minutes, then turned back up the hill. There was no main road here, only a jumble of houses and mosques

142

through which some narrow lanes led upwards. I caught a glimpse of a minaret wrapped in scaffolding on my left, took the next left turning and soon found myself running along a high wall below the mosque. I ran right round it twice, but could not recognise the road to our hotel. I was not quite at the panic stage, but I recalled that our hotel was very small, I had no idea what its street was called, and the room-key in my pocket gave no clues. My leisurely pace became more determined. I was on a ridge, so I decided to run along it to the left, then to the right. By this stage I could see my breakfast slipping away... I noticed another white mosque, scaffolding round each minaret, far to my left and hurried towards it. Fortunately I spotted the road to our hotel and managed to cool down, shower and eat before "On the bus" time. From that morning on I noticed that many other mosques were white and had scaffolding round their minarets; either they are high maintenance or I had chanced on the Minaret Repair Season.

I discovered a fellow runner in the tour party, Allan, so we ran together the next morning. This time we crossed the Golden Horn by one bridge, ran along the far bank and crossed back on the lower bridge. It was chilly in the early morning, but both bridges were lined with fishermen, each with a long spinning-rod. We had to run very carefully as these chaps were not used to runners, and would turn, walk backwards, gather in groups and lay rods down. It was worth it, however, to see them leaning over the parapet fishing. Some caught small fish which they kept alive in plastic buckets, but one or two stood proudly beside buckets with larger fish. There were so many fishermen that I feared for the crew of any boat passing below—it must have looked to them like a curtain of nylon lines as they approached the bridge. There were two plus points to this run; firstly Allan and I did not get lost, and secondly we found our running speeds to be compatible.

After Istanbul we visited Gallipolli, and crossed the Dardanelles before checking in at a waterfront hotel at Canakkale. From the hotel in Asia we looked over the water to Europe. A path by the shore was so enticing that my wife joined me for a run before dinner. It was a bright, calm evening; ships sailed serenely past and the clear water lapped peacefully at our feet. This was some contrast to the scene in 1915, when Allied Forces failed to break the defences of the Turks. Several British and French warships were sunk in the narrows where we ran. Our visit earlier that day to the battle sites came one week before ANZAC Day, when New Zealand and Australian visitors would come to pay respects to their dead.

Our next two nights were in a quaint hotel overlooking the bay of Kusadasi. Allan and I arranged to meet for an early run on the first morning. We ran down to the waterfront, then right along the bay to a small island with a fort at the far end. The walls of the fort started at sea level, and a quick exploration confirmed that an attempt to run round the island might result in a bit of swimming. Instead we chose to climb to a monument on the headland which offered a fine view over the town. The climb started on a concrete track but soon we were "off-piste" on rabbit tracks and through holes in fences. The view was excellent, but we did not linger, threading our way down via steep paths and steps to the main waterfront, and back to our hotel. It was good to look over the bay to see where we had been, and our effort earned some respect from members of the tour party.

We had a long day of travel and two heavy sessions of sightseeing between Kusidasi and Pamukkale. The only large hotel in the district was designed in blocks (we were in Block 5) and it was packed, the dinner buffet buzzing with visitors from all over the world. Allan and I met at 7 the next morning and headed up a track which disappeared up a wooded hillside. It was a crisp morning, and we saw no-one, a delightful contrast to our hotel which, as Allan said, could double as a prison if it failed as an hotel. As our track climbed higher and higher we were able to see magnificent, snow-covered peaks across the valley in sharp focus in the clear morning air. After half an hour or so we turned for home, passing a thermal spring which gushed steam at us, and reaching the hotel as a tour bus pulled away, belching smoke. We were back from our peaceful escape—tourists once again.

In Antalya we stayed two nights in the splendid Dedeman Hotel, on a cliff above the Aegean Sea. Our guide had told us we were not far from one of the two main beaches, so on our first morning Allan and I set off at 7 to explore to the right, hoping for a canter along a beach-side promenade. We started along a promising road which followed the line of the cliffs. It opened into a wide grassy area, pleasant to run through. Sadly we soon reached the far end and found chain-link fencing which protected the grounds of another hotel. At the cliff end we managed to wriggle round the fencing, and ran through the grounds. A guard started walking purposefully behind us, but we outpaced him and shinned over the fence at the far end into a narrow street. By now we were aware that the beach was probably not in this direction, but agreed to run on to a headland with a small lighthouse which we could see in the middle distance. The direct line took us through more areas where visitors appeared to be discouraged. When we reached the lighthouse we could see the coastline ahead. There was definitely no beach—line after line of cliffs with tall buildings close to the edge, so we cut our losses and headed back for breakfast. For the return we opted for a small road between our cliff-top route and the main road, and were surprised to find a narrow jogging track at one side of it. We met several runners, and, in the international camaraderie of runners, greeted them with Good Morning in Turkish: "Guneiden!" This run lasted a good hour, and was very enjoyable after the long days in the bus. Allan's stories to tour members of my choice of route ensured that my reputation for finding "interesting" runs was enhanced. The coach departed very early next morning, so we had no chance to explore to the left of the hotel.

There followed two hard days of travel with no opportunity for a run, but our last night was back in the original Istanbul hotel, and Allan and I were determined to end the tour on a running high. At 6.45 we met in the foyer and set off down the opposite slope of the ridge to the Golden Horn. We ran down until we reached the dual carriageway which skirts the Bosphorus. It was a beautiful morning, but cool, which is why we politely declined the invitation to join some bathers who were undressing on the rocks. With the famous waterway on our right we ran past familiar landmarks above us on the left—The Blue Mosque, Aya Sophia and Topkapi, all places we had visited and enjoyed. At the bend in the road we left the Bosphorus and ran along the bank of the Golden Horn. We viewed the decaying façade of the railway station, famous as the terminus of the Orient Express. After a splendid mosque (white with scaffolded minarets!) we reached the Spice Market and swung left to brave the steep, bustling alleys which led up to our ridge. We did not exactly get lost, but there was a time when we were unsure of our exact position... To be absolutely sure we took a detour to a mosque to confirm that it was Suleiman's, then we trotted back to our hotel with confidence.

The problems with running while on a tour are mainly those of timing and logistics. With a packed programme it is difficult to find time for a run in the mornings: "Cases outside your rooms at 7.30, ready to leave at 8.15" was a frequent call, and there were few evenings when we had time for a run before dinner. With (at times) one night only in a hotel the problem of washing and drying running kit needs no explanation. Some locations, such as that of our hotel in Ankara, would encourage only the most desperate runner to brave the crowds, pollution and narrow streets. But the opportunities make it well worth facing up to the problems! As far as health is concerned a brisk run is a balance to the long hours in the coach, and to the "death by eating" of the tour party buffet meals. As an expression of freedom and adventure in a strange country the chance to run guide-less is a pure delight. At the end of our tour fellow passengers were asking each other what day, what site of antiquity or what scenery had been the highlight. I answered that Aphrodisias had been rather special, but by reading this account you will probably realise that my running, be it alone, with my wife or with Allan, had been the real highlight for me.

Exploring Almaty

David

ALMATY WAS ALMA-ATA in my school atlas; it may not be the capital of Kazakhstan, but it is by far the largest city. In fact, you could say that it is two cities. Most of the lower city is a grid pattern of drab Soviet-style tenement blocks, with the odd park thrown in, but the higher ground has wide streets with modern, grandiose buildings which reflect the way the country is developing and exploiting its mineral wealth. Hotel Inter-Continental is high above the old town and is a wonderful base for a runner. Its 18 storeys of pink concrete and blue reflective glass make an excellent landmark, visible from far away.

Unfortunately I was staying downtown in Hotel Kazkhol, a six-storey building in the centre of a small square of eight-storey tenements, tricky to find after a long run. One of my (non-runner) colleagues could not understand the problem. "It's a simple grid system," he said, "every street is at right angles. All you have to do is keep a count of the blocks you run past, take two lefts or rights and you should be one block away from the hotel." With me, it doesn't work like that. I like to follow my instincts; an interesting prospect on the left, an inviting park on the right, a market, road works... anything can cause me to lose the discipline of "right-angle" running.

My first run went to plan; I had walked much of the route along the pedestrian zone the previous day and wanted to see it from a runner's perspective. In the cold weather there were not many strollers and I enjoyed my run past gold shops, money-changing booths and cafes. I had to cross two boulevards by plunging down into subways, but had no difficulty returning to Gogol Street, which led to the hotel.

One of the problems on my second run was snow. It had fallen silently overnight and lay on road and pavement all day. When I stepped out after work for a run it was beginning to thaw, and pavements were tricky with pools of slush. I failed to respond to a warning toot from a vehicle coming up behind me and was liberally sprayed with slush from a fast-moving snowplough. I found a park and opted to run round it, as the snow was purer and drier away from the street. This was a very interesting park, dedicated to WW2's Soviet General Panfilov and the 28 Kazakh heroes who held their ground in the face of a German offensive in the Siege of Moscow in November 1941. The park also contained an ancient church, which was one of the few buildings in the city to survive the earthquakes of 1887 and 1910. By the time I had cruised past all the statues and buildings in the park darkness had fallen and I had lost my orientation. I could only remember that my hotel lay downhill from the park, and probably to the left. I headed downhill. To escape from a busy street without a pavement I ran through a fruit and vegetable market, an incongruous figure amongst the shoppers in my bright yellow cagoule. Tiring of the curious stares, I headed for a quieter street and enjoyed the peace. The unbroken snow should have warned me that it was a dead-end, but I missed a sign, if there was one. When I reached the end I saw a narrow lane on the right parallel to my road, but 2 metres lower. An exciting balancing act saw me cross the wall and drop down into the lane. A well-used path through the snow gave encouragement, until I came to a manned barrier. Fortunately I could see that this was the entry into a car park, and that there was an exit lower down. With a cheerful wave to the armed guard and no drop in pace I crossed the park as though it were routine. I soon found myself back on a major boulevard which could have been Gogol, but for the tram lines along the centre. Gogol did not have trams. I risked a further block downhill, and at the next intersection looked long and hard left and right. In the distance to the left was a building which looked familiar, a domed marble structure in the centre of the road. I recognised it from my walk as the public hall which marked the far end of the pedestrian zone. Gogol and my hotel lay beyond it. I ran past it in a mixture of triumph and relief, and 20 minutes later was in my room, giving my running shoes a quick blast from the hairdryer.

My third and final run in Almaty was on a free afternoon, when I headed up to the newer part of town. Most of the snow had vanished, and I enjoyed warm sunlight, albeit with dust blown up in a stiff breeze. In the distance I could see the jagged peaks of the Tien Shan Range, where a flourishing ski centre caters for the well-to-do. The higher I climbed, the more luxurious the buildings. Banks were well-represented, hotels, museums and public buildings with high security. Apartment blocks were light years ahead of the down-town tenements, all glass and balconies overlooking the city. A shopping mall with car park could have been in any US city. Even the parks up here displayed wealth, with formal hedge-lined gardens, fountains and ornate modern statues. Perhaps it was inevitable that my eye was drawn to the Union Jack outside the John Bull Pub with its mock-Tudor exterior; final proof the Almaty had "come of age". Returning to my hotel from here in daylight was easy, as I had a football stadium, a huge Chinese restaurant and a prominent Mercedes dealership as way-markers.

We left Almaty after an interesting week. My colleagues had used our free time to shop, while I opted to go for runs. I'm sure that I had the richer experience, not just because I had covered more of the city's streets and parks, but also because I had enjoyed the "get home" challenge of running alone in an unknown and fascinating city.

FAR EAST

Early Morning in Guilin

David

IN THE BUS FROM THE AIRPORT I spotted the Seven Stars Park, and noted that it was less than one kilometre of bustling street from our hotel. Our group had free time that afternoon, so I jogged to the park, only to find there was an entrance fee, and I had no money with me, so was not allowed in. "It's free every morning until 7 a.m.," I was told, so I finished a gentle street jog and resolved to check the park out the next morning.

At 6 a.m. it was pitch black, but the gates were open wide and people—mainly elderly—were streaming in. The park consists of seven steep-sided rocky hills, each about 250m high, and some small lakes, trees, flower beds and pagodas. Most of the other people in the park practised tai qi, some with wooden swords, or exercised through stretching, walking or gentle trotting. As darkness gave way to the pre-dawn light, I jogged carefully along the criss-crossing paths, eventually finding one which led up to a hilltop. It stopped at a pagoda two-thirds up the hill, but I could make out a rough continuation, which I followed. The path became a dark, narrow thread in a steep bank of prickly bushes, then stopped abruptly at the foot of a cliff. Easy hand- and footholds invited me to keep going, and I hauled my way up the cliff to emerge on the broad summit just as dawn broke.

A svelte female figure stood on the highest point, facing away from me. I advanced towards the centre of the summit, and was just about to give a polite warning cough when she yelled. It came from way down, it was very loud and it went on, and on, and on. I stood rooted to the spot. She bent low, then straightened and drew breath. Another yell started, and again I felt distinctly uneasy. Had she spotted me climbing, and was she feeling threatened? Had I trespassed onto *her* hilltop?

When she bent down to start her third yell I heard an answering yell from another hilltop, and then another. Puzzled, I settled down a discreet distance from the yelling lady, and enjoyed a spectacular sunrise. From all over the park protracted yells sounded, and then it clicked! The solitary yellers were exercising their lungs, and had sought out isolated spots where they would not cause a noise nuisance to other park users. My lady went on yelling for several minutes, then disappeared down the cliff. Alone on my summit, I tried it. Gentle yells to begin with, then louder, finally full volume, and do you know what?—I really enjoyed it!

Back in the hotel I joined the rest of my group for the breakfast buffet scrum, then visited the spectacular sights of Guilin. Long after the memory of the magnificent scenery fades, my little early morning adventure will stay fresh in my mind.

Hong Kong: Running Wild

David

IN THE SEVENTIES AND EIGHTIES I lived in Hong Kong for a total of six years, and running became a favourite activity. Beyond the noisy, concrete jungle lay peaceful hills and valleys with some excellent trails where you could run on your own for hours.

Not all runs were straightforward, however. Straying off the main paths in thickly wooded areas could lead to some challenging jungle-bashing; a minor path leading in the direction you wanted could end abruptly at a hillside grave, but who wants to go back down to the main path? Continuing to run in the same direction through bamboo thickets, over rocky stream beds with lush vegetation, was not for the fainthearted. The thought often crossed my mind: Who would ever find me if I had a problem here? I knew that the answer was—probably—no-one.

Large spiders added an unpleasant moment or two to some runs. How they managed it, I don't know, but they could build webs across a trail, so that the early morning jogger could run into the web at face height. If the spider happened to be on the web at the time, it would no doubt be angry that its hard work had been spoiled, and might wish to vent its anger by biting the intruder. I don't know much about spiders, but these were large black fellows with prominent yellow spots, so I conclude that their lack of camouflage stems from their ability to look after themselves. Wild pigs, though they avoid contact with people when possible, could also be a danger if panicked by a soft-footed runner. I caused several to crash through the undergrowth at my approach.

I saw several snakes while out running, but avoided any confrontations. Some were in monsoon drains, well below my feet, others slithered across a trail ahead of me. If I felt that I had trespassed into a snake area, I would sometimes roll a stone into long grass ahead of me as a warning of my presence.

Wild dogs were not really a problem. They existed, of course, but the trick with dogs is to bend down and make as if you are picking up a stone, and raise your throwing arm. They back off quickly enough. The same could not be said for the guard dogs which were let out for exercise behind some of the hillside homes of the rich. They were best avoided.

Anyway, this story is not about dogs, it is about baboons.

When I lived in Kowloon Tong, I had a great run which never failed to delight me. I ran up Broadcast Drive and turned off the busy road onto a rutted track which led through a shanty town to a well-built, ancient path in what is now Lion Rock Park. With the last shack behind me, the harsh gray gave way to green, and the noise of the city receded with every step. The worn stones led upwards at a gentle angle to the col to the west of Lion Rock. The path continued over to Amah Rock and Shatin, but I turned left on gaining the ridge and jogged towards Beacon Hill at the far end. This part of the run was fantastic! Far below, Hong Kong clanged, hooted and hammered; boats criss-crossed the harbour, streams of cars flowed along Nathan Road and

Boundary Street, and one jet after another aimed at a red and white checked marker on a hillside below me, then—right hand down a bit!—straightened up to land at Kai Tak Airport. This run was the best way to slough off the rigours of a hard day's work at the office.

There is a weather radar station at the high point of Beacon Hill. There is a "golf ball" radar installation and a separate concrete building with masts at the head of a concrete access road, the Lung Fan Road, which leads down to Kowloon. The smooth surface of the road means that you can lope down, without having to keep your eyes cast downwards for hazards, and there are some superb views to enjoy.

At one point the road curves north into a cutting through the soft red rock, then it resumes its southerly direction until it reaches the Yuen Long Highway.

On one occasion I sped down the road towards the cutting as usual, but as I turned the bend I saw immediately in front of me, on the road and on the verges, a large troop of baboons. The scene had the appearance of an assembly, or business meeting. Even after braking hard I was amongst them before I could stop. They all seemed to flinch, and there were one or two snarls. Instinctively I bent down for the imaginary stone—as for the dogs—but this was a bad choice. There are colonies of baboons in Hong Kong which are popular attractions for local and foreign visitors, but the creatures are often persecuted by small boys with stones, and my threatening gesture did not go down well. They all glared and snarled at me now, baring their long, yellow fangs and crouching, ready to spring. I held my arm in the "prepare to throw" position and eased my way through the troop, rather like the gunslinger with drawn pistol escaping from the hostile saloon, twisting and turning to cover an attack from each direction. One or two of them lunged at me threateningly, but none made contact. Once clear of the outer fringe I continued walking backwards downhill until out of sight.

I ran that route for several months afterwards, and every time crept round that bend in tense expectation, but never saw a single baboon there again.

I am going back next year. No illusions that things will be as they were twenty years ago, but I will climb up to the ridge and jog along to Beacon Hill.

Wonder if there will be any baboons to greet me?

Hong Kong Snake

David

IT WAS SUNDAY; the first day of sun and blue sky after a week of heavy rain, and I just had to go for a run.

I knew the route well; starting with a steep climb out of Repulse Bay, it contours round the hillside and descends to a remote reservoir. At the far end there was a decision to be made: either carry on down the track to the main road and return along the flat tarmac, or climb to the top of the hill and go down a steep, stony path to the start point.

It was a good feeling to be out on such a fine day! I puffed my way up the worn path until I reached the monsoon ditch, then relaxed as I jogged along its flat concrete lip. After 2km I reached the metalled road which links two reservoirs and stretched my legs for a pleasant downhill canter down to Tai Tam. It was the time and place to consider my two options, but the decision came very quickly. It was definitely a day for the hilltop! I turned off the track onto a narrow path which led relentlessly up to the summit. The going was good, as the red earth had dried quickly, and in some places flat stones had been bedded into the path to form a crude stairway. Once again I changed gear into my off-road speed, and, with head down to pick my way over stones, I made steady progress to the top. It would have been a crime not to stop and admire the view, so stop I did. The water of the South China Sea sparkled beneath me.

Container ships glided and fishing boats bustled in the channel, while yachts and windsurfers criss-crossed Stanley Bay. I could hear the traffic below, but the convex slope kept the vehicles out of sight. I had the hill to myself, a rare, peaceful moment in busy Hong Kong.

Eventually I set off down the far side of the hill. The path was steep but well-designed, and I was able to leap from one strategically-placed stone to the next. I soon built up a good speed, with one foot on one stone, the other foot aimed at the second one, and the eyes looking for the third and fourth. Halfway down the slope my eyes chose a large flat stone in the centre of the path and I plotted it into my course. To my horror I then saw that a large grey snake (probably a rat snake) was coiled on the top of the stone! It, too, was enjoying the sun after the rain. As I spotted it, it heard or saw me. It probably realised in a flash that a Size 9 Pegasus was about to land on its stone, whether it protested or not! To this day I can see in my mind how it uncoiled and threw itself into the bushes at the side of the path just before I hit that stone! Without turning round to watch its escape I carried on—a little slower, with a regular glance down the path for other sunbathing snakes, but there were none.

Reaching the road, I was back in the "concrete jungle" with building sites and traffic noise. My short escapes to the natural world, even this one with the near-miss snake encounter, were for me the icing on the cake to life in Hong Kong.

The Shortcut

David

I WAS A MEMBER OF A SMALL DELEGATION on a strenuous tour of secondary schools in south-east China. What made the tour hard work was that each school laid on a banquet for us, at breakfast, lunchtime or in the evening, and on a couple of days that meant all three! I could see the risk to health so adopted a no-booze strategy. I had no problem here, as I had convinced our Chinese minder that I was on medical advice not to touch the stuff. He interpreted this as meaning that I was a reformed alcoholic, and our hosts took his hint not to force it on me. Food was a different matter! Well-meaning chopsticks placed delicacy after delicacy onto my plate, and I did my diplomatic best to appreciate them. Crab was usually a highlight, spoilt only by our minder's pronunciation ("Have a crap..."). It follows that running became an essential balance to the rich diet, and I ran early in the morning whenever I could.

Our leader was an old China hand, and he had sensibly fitted three days of rest halfway through the tour. We had visited a school in Guilin on a Thursday, then we said goodbye to our minder and boarded a tourist boat on the Li River, to chug through the spectacular landscape of karst rock formations upstream to Yangshuo. This small town has become a delightful tourist resort, partly because it was as far upstream as the steamers could go, and partly for the awesome scenery of terraced rice fields and dramatic sheer-sided mountains. At the quay there is a road along the bank of the river, and, at right-angles, West Street leads away from the river and forms the spine of the town. It offers stall after stall of souvenirs, clothes, leather goods, music and artwork, while much of the street behind these stalls is taken up by small hotels. We booked into the excellent Sihai Hotel, and promenaded up and down the bustling street before an austere supper and an early bed.

The next morning I slipped into my running kit and crept out of the hotel very early. The sky was a deep blue, the streets deserted and I settled into a leisurely running pace. No need to rush back for the minder waiting at the minibus, the whole day was mine. What a wonderful feeling of release! Being familiar with the eastern end of West Street where it meets the riverside, I turned west. Yangshuo is a small town, and I soon found myself running into the countryside between wheat fields with fantastic views in all directions. After 40 minutes of carefree running I noted that the road had turned north and was starting to climb gently to a gap between two rounded, tree-covered hills. That suited me; it would go over the gap and cut down to the Li River again, so I could simply take the riverside road back to the town. I attacked the hill and paused, panting, at the crest. I looked down to the Li River valley and registered two points. Firstly I was alone in beautiful weather at a view-point with as magnificent a panorama as I have seen anywhere, and, secondly, my road did not descend to the river as I had thought, but curled gently up and over the hill on my left, away from Yangshuo. I could see the far bank of the river, but a steep convex slope of scraggy bushes and trees prevented me from seeing my own bank. The sensible thing to do would have been to retrace my steps back along the road, a pleasant downhill trot, then an easy jog back to the hotel and breakfast.

However... I peered down, looking for a path heading south-east which would take me downstream towards Yangshuo. This shortcut would link up with the road and probably bring me back to the hotel a little sooner. There was no path, but surely I would meet one on the slope... With a last sweep of the eyes over the dramatic horizon I left the road and set off down the hillside. I had to concentrate, as the ground was a mixture of rocks and sun-baked, gritty clods. The easy slope at the top gave way to a steeper section with thicker bushes, and running became boulder-hopping, sliding and scrambling. Heavy rain at some stage had created v-shaped ravines which slowed me down; I had to concentrate hard on foot placement and keeping branches from my face. After a particularly difficult stretch I paused and looked around me. Apart from some bright yellow butterflies in the dappled sunlight there were no signs of life. Looking ahead down the slope I was shocked to see—not 15 metres ahead—the swiftly-flowing, green water of the river. There was no riverside road after all! I descended carefully down to the edge and hopped onto some stones just off the bank. The river was about 50m wide with a strong current; to me it seemed full of menace. Downstream, where I was heading, I could see the river curving sharply to the left, and my bank became a steep wall of dense woodland. Just then I heard the sound of a vehicle on the far bank, and saw a small truck pottering along through the trees. So the road engineer had decided to cross the river, either by ferry or bridge, rather than build along my steep bend! I had a problem.

There seemed to be three options: firstly to go back the way I had come, secondly to swim or float down river, and thirdly to carry on along my bank. The first was not for this day of freedom, the second was, well..., only if really desperate, so I decided to carry on.

I remember clearly the difficulties I faced but will not go into detail. Suffice to say, I battled with nature in the form of spiky, "impenetrable" bushes which I had to penetrate or go round, and gravity, as the steep, slope of crumbly rock threatened to send me down to the river at any point. I became very hot and sticky, and started muttering to myself. As I overcame one problem, another presented itself. I could not wade along the bank, as the water flowed swift and deep as it rounded the bend, and I could not climb high, as the upper slope was a sheer rock face. Eventually I reached a small banana grove, next a farm, a track, then finally a road which started at a ferry ramp and took me back to Yangshuo. I staggered up the steps to the Sihai three hours after I had left it, showered and breakfasted, then sat on the veranda to watch the world go by. Confident in the knowledge that our minder was 40 miles away back in Guilin, I then sank several beers.

Round the West Lake

David

IT WAS 22nd OCTOBER and we were sipping Dragon Well tea at the Leaping Tiger Pavilion at China's West Lake.

An hour earlier I had booked in to the prestigious Hangzhou Overseas Chinese Hotel—all sumptuous red walls, gold-painted lions and marble—and had met my friend Nanyi Guan, with whom I had taught in Edinburgh a few years earlier. I had shown him many of Scotland's attractions, and he was delighted to be my guide in Hangzhou. "It's payback time," he said in his faultless English.

Surrounded by wooded hills, West Lake has been one of China's most popular beauty spots for centuries. Low bridges and tall pagodas complement the natural beauty, and the place has historical importance, too. Hangzhou is famous as the centre for China's silk industry, and Chairman Mao loved this lake and the local Dragon Well tea. He worked on the draft constitution of the new People's Republic here in 1953.

We strolled back to the hotel along a broad cycle and pedestrian track, and I asked Nanyi if the path we were on went right round the lake. He knew that it did, as it is a favourite cycle trip for him and his wife, about 20-22 kilometres long, he said. "I can run that," I thought, and did some calculating. I had to drive to Yiwu next day... best leave Hangzhou at 9 a.m. .... I'll need over two hours for the run... wash, pack, take breakfast...

"I'm going to run round the lake tomorrow morning," I told Nanyi, "starting at 5 a.m." Nanyi was astounded that anyone should want to run round the lake, especially at that time of the late autumn morning, but immediately promised that he would come with me on his bike before starting his day at school.

At the appointed hour he was at the front entrance to the hotel, astride his sit-up-and-beg bike. In the wicker basket strapped to the handlebars he had water, bread and watermelon for me. We set off together in pre-dawn early morning mist and found a pace which was brisk enough for us to keep warm, yet easy enough for us to continue our catching-up chat of the previous day. The air was pleasantly still and cool, and we soon left the town behind us. A gentle light allowed us to see the outlines of the hills, and before too long we could make out the features of our surroundings. We had chosen to go round anti-clockwise, so had lake views and strips of tall reeds on our left and vegetable fields and houses on our right. After 40 minutes we reached a causeway which curved across the lake. Nanyi, being one of those who can't see the point of running after the invention of the bicycle, reckoned that I had done enough, and steered me towards it. I was feeling strong, however, and asked him to carry on round the main lake. With a shake of the head he turned back onto our path, and started feeding me slices of watermelon (delicious on a run!). I passed on the bread. We made steady progress, and I enjoyed one of those special, serene passages of time when you are fully aware that there is nothing else you would rather be doing.

At 6.15 a.m. I recognised the building ahead of me. Without a doubt it was the Leaping Tiger Pavilion, no more than 500m from the hotel, and yet I had only been running for an hour and a quarter! I gave Nanyi a reproachful look, as I had geared myself up for a longer run. At our pace we must have covered no more that 13km. We could have had an extra hour's sleep!

We said our farewells at the hotel entrance; he went off to teach and I left Hangzhou, perhaps never to return. I have travelled widely and this was not the first time that local estimates of distance have proved to be inaccurate. I conclude that many people don't care much about measuring distance beyond saying "long" or "far" as opposed to "near" or "short", or by measuring distance in time.

It may have been shorter than I expected, but it had been a great run and I would not have missed it for all the tea in China!

The entire royalties from the sale of this book will go to Tong-Len, a charity for street children in Northern India. It was founded by an Edinburgh family who saw them and decided to do something. Direct contact can be made at www.tong-len.org

Lightning Source UK Ltd.
Milton Keynes UK
UKOW031201180912

199203UK00001B/1/P